THE QUILTER'S HOME
Winter

D0580220

LOIS KRUSHINA FLETCHER

Martingale®
& COMPANY

CREDITS

President · *Nancy J. Martin*
CEO · *Daniel J. Martin*
Publisher · *Jane Hamada*
Editorial Director · *Mary V. Green*
Managing Editor · *Tina Cook*
Technical Editor · *Laurie Baker*
Copy Editor · *Melissa Bryan*
Design Director · *Stan Green*
Illustrator · *Laurel Strand*
Cover and Text Designer · *Trina Stahl*
Photographer · *Brent Kane*

That Patchwork Place® is an imprint of
Martingale & Company®.

The Quilter's Home: Winter
© 2003 by Lois Krushina Fletcher

Martingale & Company
20205 144th Avenue NE
Woodinville, WA 98072-8478 USA
www.martingale-pub.com

Printed in China
08 07 06 05 04 03   8 7 6 5 4 3 2

MISSION STATEMENT

*Dedicated to providing quality products and service
to inspire creativity.*

Library of Congress Cataloging-in-Publication Data

Fletcher, Lois Krushina.
    The quilter's home : winter / Lois Krushina Fletcher.
        p. cm.
    ISBN 1-56477-476-7
1. Patchwork—Patterns. 2. Quilting. 3. Winter in art.
I. Title.
    TT835.F57625 2003
    746.46'041—dc21

                                            2002156262

DEDICATION

To my wonderful husband, Judge, who keeps my head in the clouds and gives me wings to fly.

ACKNOWLEDGMENTS

Special thanks go to Mary Burton, Ginger Hellsten, Michelle Hale, Judy Danz, Cindy Imdieke, Kathy Alaniz, Sherry Moore, Georgeanne Pinson, and Shannon Coutant for testing some of the patterns in this book. Their feedback was invaluable and they tolerated my never getting things to them when I said I would.

I would also like to thank the following fabric manufacturers for their generous help in acquiring just the right fabrics for the projects in this book: Fabric Traditions, Timeless Treasures, Robert Kaufman, and a special thanks to Northcott Monarch for providing the perfect border fabric for "Winter."

My thanks once again to Martingale & Company for their enthusiasm and support. Their editors and staff are truly a joy to work with.

Finally, words cannot begin to express my appreciation and thanks to my husband, Judge, for his hard work to support me while I pursue my career. He endures endless evenings at home and countless "no's" when he wants to take me out, and he never complains when I remind him of my deadlines. He is also my number-one fan.

CONTENTS

INTRODUCTION

WINTER. THE MERE word evokes thoughts of ice and snow. The frosty air, filled with delicate snowflakes falling to the ground, creates a frozen playground. Soon there will be snowmen in every yard, children ice skating and sledding, and the crunch of snow underfoot. What a wonderful time of year. Even as nature sleeps, there's such beauty to behold and fun to be had.

If you love the magic of winter, then this wall hanging is designed for you. Think you're not "good" enough? Don't be intimidated by how difficult it may look. All of the appliqués use fusible web and the step-by-step block instructions take you through the construction process by completing one block at a time. Not proficient with your satin stitching? Use a small zigzag stitch with invisible nylon thread instead. You won't see the stitches and your projects will still look stunning. Short on time? Create your own block-of-the-month! If you make just one block each month, the 11 unique blocks plus the Friendship Stars will take you through the year with little time expenditure on your part. Before you know it, you will have all your blocks ready to complete this spectacular wall hanging.

In this book you will also find instructions for several home-decor items. Each item uses one or more of the designs from the "Winter" wall hanging, so they will automatically coordinate. You can make these projects with the same fabrics used in the wall hanging, or give them a different look by incorporating other fabrics. Fabric colors are listed for each project so that you can easily identify where each fabric is used, but do not feel obligated to use the same color selection. Substitute fabrics to suit your own tastes or to use whatever fabrics are in your stash. (You *do* have a stash, don't you?) The appliqués can be satin stitched with cotton thread, like most of the samples throughout the book, or you can use rayon thread to give them a bit of shimmer and a more "formal" appearance. If you prefer a country or old-fashioned look, use a buttonhole stitch with contrasting thread. You can even use metallic thread for a certain kind of elegance, as in the "Winter" mantel banner on page 52. Whichever way you choose to make them, the projects are sure to incorporate a beautiful seasonal theme throughout your home.

If you are familiar with my first book, *The Quilter's Home: Fall*, you may notice that many of the blocks in this book are the same dimensions. This was no accident. With just a little imagination, you can substitute many of the blocks from one book into the projects from the other. This increases your decorating options even more!

All of the projects in this book use either fusible-web appliqué, paper piecing, or a combination of the two in the construction process. The instructions for these techniques are presented in "Basic Techniques" on pages 7–11, so be sure to read through that section before embarking on any of the projects, even if you are already familiar with the processes.

When you are ready to complete your projects, turn to "Project Finishing" on pages 12–15. There you will find helpful advice for marking, layering, quilting, and binding your projects.

BASIC TECHNIQUES

I
N THIS SECTION, I describe techniques for making the blocks required for the projects in this book. Every quilter has her (or his) own way of doing things, so even if you are already accomplished at fusible-web appliqué and paper piecing, please take the time to read this section so you will be familiar with how I have presented the patterns and instructions.

TESTING FOR ACCURACY

The object when machine piecing is to sew with a scant ¼" seam allowance. The reason for this is that the bulk of the seams, especially when pressed to one side, take up some of the fabric with their loft. If the seam measured exactly ¼", the finished piece would be too small. Even a slight difference in the size of the seam allowance can have a big impact on the final results. That is why the following test for accuracy is so important.

When testing your sewing machine for accuracy, use a ¼" foot if your machine has one. Although ¼" feet are made with quilters and machine piecing in mind, they do not necessarily give you the perfect scant ¼" seam allowance you need. If you discover that yours does not, try using other feet and/or needle positions, or try aligning the edge of the fabric at a slightly different position under the foot. I personally use my all-purpose foot with the needle position one click to the right, as I find this gives me greater accuracy than my ¼" foot. Experiment until you find the best presser foot, needle position, and/or guide to give you the most accurate possible seam allowance.

To test your stitching for accuracy, do the following:

1. Cut 3 strips of fabric, each 1½" x 3".

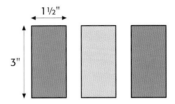

2. Sew the strips together along the long edges using a scant ¼" seam allowance. Press the seams to one side and measure the piece. Its width should now measure exactly 3½", and the center strip should measure exactly 1" across. If it does not, adjust your presser foot or needle position and repeat the test.

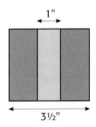

FUSIBLE-WEB APPLIQUÉ

One of the greatest developments in the world of quilting has to be the invention of paper-backed fusible web. It has opened up a whole new world to quilters who might never have tried the art of machine appliqué otherwise. I should know: I am one of them. In the beginning, only one type of fusible web was available, but with competition and demand came improvements. Now there are many different types to choose from, but for the projects in this book, select a lightweight web that you can sew through. (Do not attempt to use any fusible web that is separating from the paper! It is a waste of time and effort.)

When using fusible webs, prewash your fabrics. Fabrics are coated with sizing, which could potentially keep the adhesive from sticking properly. For that same reason, do not use fabric softeners of any kind, even dryer sheets, when prewashing and drying your fabrics.

One of the most important things to remember about fusible-web appliqué is that the appliqué design must be the reverse of the image on the finished design. All the appliqué patterns in this book have already been reversed. If you are using hand-appliqué methods, you will need to make mirror-image appliqué patterns and add turn-under allowances.

To make the appliqués for the projects in this book:

1. Follow the project instructions to trace the indicated appliqué patterns onto the paper side of the fusible web, leaving a small amount of space between each shape. Most of the appliqués are shown as they will be arranged on the background piece, which means some shapes will be overlapping others. To distinguish each individual appliqué, the outline of each pattern is shown in a different color than the shape(s) next to it. To trace the individual appliqués, follow the same color line, whether it is a solid line or a series of long dashed lines. The long dashed lines simply indicate where shapes overlap. You will refer to the lines when assembling the appliqué units, so make sure to trace them onto the appliqué shape. Any short dashed lines indicate detail stitching; you do not need to trace them onto the fusible web. Be sure to mark the pattern letter on each piece, because you will assemble the appliqué shapes in alphabetical order.

2. Cut out the traced shapes leaving a ⅛" margin. On large pieces, such as the snowman and ice-skate patterns, cut away the inner portion of the fusible-web shape to eliminate bulk and/or the background fabric showing through. Gently fold the fusible-web piece in half and make a small snip in the middle of the fold. Insert the tip of the scissors through the hole and cut ¼" to ⅜" from the inner edges.

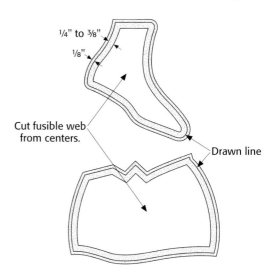

3. Follow the manufacturer's instructions to fuse the appliqué shapes to the wrong side of the appropriate fabrics.

4. Cut out the appliqué shapes on the drawn lines. Gently peel away the paper backing from the fabric.

Your appliqué shapes are now ready to be fused to the background fabric. Do not fuse each individual shape onto the background fabric. Instead, make an appliqué unit. By making an appliqué unit, you can use the placement diagram and an appliqué pressing sheet to fuse all the appliqués together first. Then you can position the fused unit on the background fabric. You will eliminate guesswork when positioning the appliqués and also

If you have difficulty getting the paper to begin peeling away from the fabric edge, lightly score the paper with the point of a pin. The paper will tear along the scored line, and you can begin the peeling process at that point. Be careful not to fray the edges of an appliqué piece by trying to force unwilling paper to separate from the fabric. The ragged edges that may result are more difficult to stitch down and might not adhere properly to the background fabric.

achieve greater accuracy when centering the design on the background fabric.

To make an appliqué unit:

1. Make a placement diagram for the project. To do this, copy or trace the appliqué patterns onto tracing or typing paper exactly as they appear on the indicated page(s). Turn the paper over and trace the image through to the blank side. A light source, such as a light box or window, makes this easier. Use the traced-through image as the placement diagram.

2. Put the placement diagram on the ironing surface. Lay the appliqué pressing sheet over the placement diagram and pin them both to the ironing-board cover with straight pins. This will prevent the layout from shifting while you are arranging the shapes.

3. Working in alphabetical order, place the appliqué shapes on the pressing sheet directly over the corresponding area on the placement diagram. The long dashed lines on the placement diagram indicate where the pieces overlap. Fuse the pieces together as they are layered on top of each other.

4. After all the pieces have been fused together, let the appliqué unit cool. Remove the unit from the pressing sheet. The fused shapes should easily peel away from the pressing sheet as one unit. If you notice some of the glue remaining on the appliqué pressing sheet as you peel off the fused unit, simply iron the unit back down and let it cool a little longer before removing.

5. Position the appliqué unit on the background fabric as indicated in the project instructions and fuse into place.

6. Refer to the appliqué patterns to mark any stitching detail lines, designated by short dashed lines, on the right side of the appliqués.

The edges of the individual appliqué shapes are now ready to be stitched down. The stitching not only secures the appliqués to the fabric, but it also prevents the appliqué edges from fraying when the project is washed or handled.

There are several ways to secure the edges. The first way is to use a satin stitch, which is a closely spaced zigzag stitch. The raw edge of the appliqué piece is aligned down the center of the stitches so that it is fully encased. For this method I prefer to use 30-weight 100% cotton thread in the needle in a color that matches the appliqué fabric, and white 60-weight 100% cotton thread in the bobbin. Loosen the upper tension slightly so that the bobbin thread pulls slightly to the underside of the appliqué. I recommend using tear-away stabilizer underneath the background fabric when satin stitching. It will eliminate puckers and help the edges of the appliqué lie smooth and flat. Carefully remove the stabilizer after the stitching is complete. While mastery of satin stitching does take some practice, especially if a lot of curves or corners are involved, the result can be very attractive and well worth the time.

A similar method of securing fusible appliqué edges is simply to use a small zigzag stitch. For this method, I use clear monofilament thread in the needle and white 60-weight 100% cotton thread in the bobbin. Once again, align the appliqué raw edges down the center of the stitches.

Lastly, there is the machine blanket stitch, or buttonhole stitch, which is becoming more widely available as a built-in stitch option on sewing machines. When done in a thread color that contrasts with the appliqué, this stitch gives the project an antique or country look. I use black 100% cotton quilting thread in the needle and black 100% cotton all-purpose thread in the bobbin for this method. One important difference when using a machine blanket stitch, as opposed to a zigzag or satin stitch, is that the appliqué raw edge is placed adjacent to the straight-stitch portion of the blanket stitch, not centered in the middle as with the other two methods.

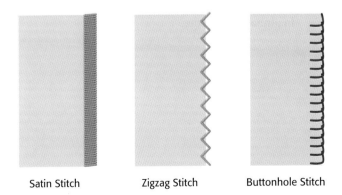

Satin Stitch   Zigzag Stitch   Buttonhole Stitch

PAPER PIECING

With paper piecing, as with any technique, there are several ways to achieve the same result. Whatever way works best for you is the "right" way. The methods described here are those that I have found, through trial and error, work best for me.

In paper piecing, the foundation pattern is the reverse image of the completed block because the block is sewn from the back of the printed pattern. The following is a brief description of how paper piecing is done. If this technique is new to you, I suggest following detailed guidelines, such as those contained in Carol Doak's *Show Me How to Paper Piece* (That Patchwork Place, 1997). There you will find step-by-step instructions for learning the technique, as well as clear photographs.

Paper Piecing Single Units

1. Photocopy or trace the foundation pattern onto a lightweight paper that provides a clear image, is easy to tear away, and does not transfer ink to the fabric.

2. The foundation sections are numbered and will be sewn in order numerically. Cut a piece of fabric big enough to cover section 1. Place the wrong side of the fabric piece against the unprinted side of the foundation pattern, making sure that it covers section 1 on all sides by at least ¼". Pin in place from the paper side.

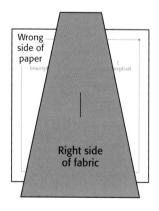

3. Turn the fabric side up. With right sides together, place a piece of fabric big enough to cover section 2 over the section 1 piece, making sure that the fabric edge extends past the line between sections 1 and 2 by at least ¼".

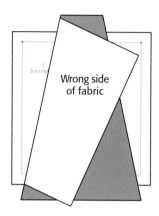

4. Reduce the stitch length on your machine to 18 to 20 stitches per inch. Holding the fabric for section 2 in place, turn the foundation unit to the paper side and stitch along the line between sections 1 and 2, beginning and ending a few stitches beyond both ends of the line. Remove the pins.

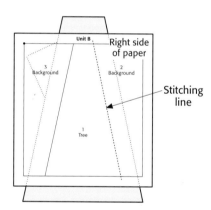

5. With the paper side up, fold back the paper along the seam line and trim the seam allowance to ¼". Turn

the foundation unit to the fabric side and press the fabric open so that it covers section 2.

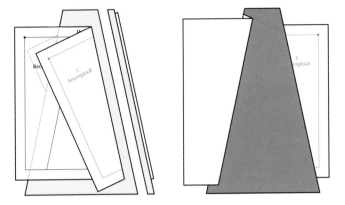

6. Repeat this process until all of the sections have been covered with fabric. Turn the completed unit to the paper side and trim the block along the outer dotted line. To prevent the bias edges from stretching when handled, do not remove the paper until the block has been set in the quilt, unless specified in the project instructions.

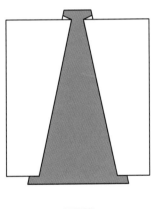

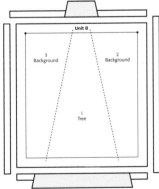

Joining Multiple Units

There are several paper-piecing foundations used throughout this book that require one or more separate paper-pieced units to be stitched together to complete the block (for example, Evergreen Tree, Winter Cabin, and Cardinal). Here's how to do it:

1. Paper piece each unit as described in the preceding section, "Paper Piecing Single Units." Be sure to mark the alignment dots and the unit letter on each pattern when tracing the foundations.

2. Push a straight pin through the first alignment dot of unit A from the *paper side*. Push the pin all the way through the fabric until the head of the pin is flush with the paper.

3. Now, push the pin through the *fabric side* of unit B so that it emerges through the corresponding alignment dot on the paper side of the unit. Push unit B up the pin to meet unit A. Make sure the pin head is still flush with the paper in unit A.

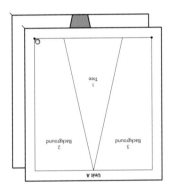

4. While holding units A and B firmly, pin them together right next to the alignment pin with a second pin, being careful not to shift the fabric layers in the process. Remove the alignment pin.

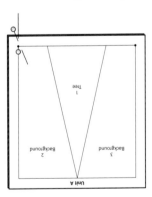

5. Repeat steps 3 and 4 with the remaining alignment dots. Stitch the 2 units together along the outer solid line of unit A. Remove the paper from the seam allowances only. Press the seam in the direction indicated in the project instructions.

Project Finishing

Whether you have made a wall hanging, a pillow sham, or a table topper, this section will help you with general finishing instructions to complete your project. Specific instructions are included with each project. All the projects in this book were machine quilted, but you may, of course, hand quilt if you prefer.

MARKING THE TOP FOR QUILTING

I like to mark all my quilting lines, except those that will be stitched in the ditch or stipple quilted. If you choose to mark the project top, you must do it *after* the completed top is pressed and *before* the top is layered. Pressing the top after it is marked could permanently set the marks.

Many suitable marking tools are available. My favorites are a fine-point mechanical pencil for light-color fabrics and, more recently, the Clover White Marking Pen for dark-color fabrics. I tried this new pen and now it is virtually the only tool I use for marking darker fabrics. It makes a very fine white line upon drying, much finer than the silver pencil that I used to use, and the lines are erasable with either water or heat. I occasionally use a water-erasable blue marker for light-color fabrics, but if you choose to use one, be prepared to dampen the marks several times to remove them, as they tend to reappear as the fabric dries. I have never had this problem when using heat to erase the white marker, but *do not use heat to erase the blue marker!* It may set the lines. Whichever marking tool you choose, be sure to test it on a scrap of fabric first to make sure the lines are removable.

ASSEMBLING THE LAYERS

The next step is to layer the top with backing and batting.

1. Cut the backing and batting at least 2" larger than the project top on all sides. In some cases, you will need to piece the backing fabric to make a large enough piece. Be sure to trim off the selvages if these edges will be seamed. Press the seam open.

2. Place the backing, wrong side up, on a clean, flat surface, such as a table or floor. Secure it on all sides with masking tape, or use 1" binder clips to fasten the backing to the table edges. The backing should be taut, but be careful not to stretch it out of shape or the finished project could pucker. Place the batting on top of the backing and smooth it in place. I find that the long edge of an acrylic ruler works better than my hand for smoothing out the batting. Lastly, place the quilt top on the batting, right side up. Center it over the batting and smooth out any wrinkles.

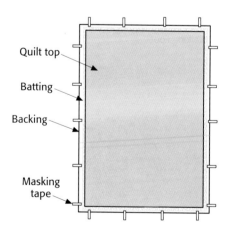

3. The backing, batting, and quilt top now need to be basted together to keep them from shifting as the project is handled and to keep the backing and batting smooth and pucker-free. The three most common basting tools are thread, safety pins, and tacks. If you are machine quilting, I recommend safety pins because you can remove them as you quilt. I prefer to use 1" safety pins. Place the pins about 4" apart in all directions. You do not need to place them in an exact grid; it is better to position them where they will not interfere with the quilting lines. It is easier to insert all of the pins first, and then go back and close them all.

QUILTING

For straight-line quilting and some in-the-ditch quilting, a walking foot is helpful. Both the top and bottom fabrics feed through this type of presser foot at the same rate, which helps to keep the layers from shifting during quilting. For any other quilting, I recommend free-motion quilting, which requires that you drop the feed dogs and use a darning foot. Once you establish the correct motor speed and the correct rate at which to move the fabric to produce a consistent stitch, free-motion quilting is just a matter of practice. The best tip I can give you is to relax your shoulders and try not to tense up. Let your movements flow naturally and your quilting lines will flow with them.

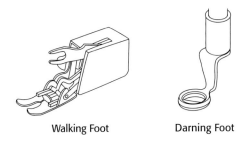

Walking Foot   Darning Foot

When it is necessary to begin or end a stitching line in the middle of a quilt, reduce the stitch length and take several very tiny stitches. The threads will be secure and can be cut flush with the top and backing of the project. Do not make several stitches in the same hole, as the threads will form a knot on the back of the quilt.

BINDING THE EDGES

I prefer a French double-fold binding, which is made using strips of fabric that are cut on grain. I do not trim the edges of my batting and backing until the binding is sewn to the project top. This gives more control over the exact amount of batting left in the seam allowance, which results in a binding that is full all the way to the fold.

To bind the project edges:

1. Cut the binding strips as indicated in the project cutting instructions.

2. Place 2 binding strips at right angles to each other, right sides together. Draw a diagonal line on the top strip where the edges of the 2 strips intersect. Stitch along the drawn line. Trim the seam allowance to ¼" and press the seam open. Repeat with any remaining strips to make 1 long strip.

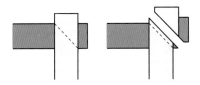

Joining Straight-Cut Binding Strips

3. Cut one end of the binding strip at a 45° angle. Press the binding strip in half lengthwise, wrong sides together and raw edges matching.

Fold line

4. Beginning with the angled end of the binding strip, align the raw edges of the strip with the raw edge of the project top. On larger projects, such as the "Winter" wall hanging, begin stitching 8" to 10" from the angled end, using a walking foot and a ¼" seam allowance. Smaller projects, such as the "Winterscape" place mats, will require less "tail" at the end. Stop ¼" from the corner of the project top; backstitch and clip the threads.

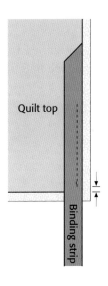

Quilt top

Binding strip

5. Turn the project so that the next seam to be sewn is in front of you. Fold the binding up to create a 45°-angle fold.

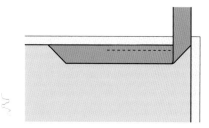

6. Fold the binding down, the fold even with the top edge of the project and the raw edges aligned with the side of the project. Beginning slightly off the edge of the binding, stitch the binding to the project, stopping ¼" from the next corner. Backstitch and clip the threads. Continue the folding and stitching process for the remaining sides.

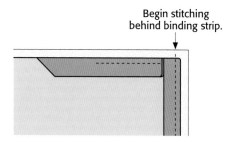

Begin stitching behind binding strip.

7. When you return to the edge where you began, end the stitching approximately 12" to 15" away from the beginning stitches; backstitch and clip the threads. (On smaller items, the distance will naturally be smaller.)

8. Lay the quilt flat and place the beginning tail on top of the ending tail. Place a mark on the ending tail where it meets the beginning tail. Place another mark ½" to the right of the first mark.

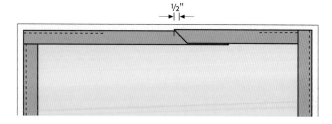

½"

9. Open out the ending tail strip and align the 45° line of a small Bias Square® ruler with the bottom edge of the opened binding strip. Place the ruler point on the mark that was ½" from the beginning tail mark. Cut the ending tail strip along the edge of the ruler as shown. The ends of both binding strips should now be cut at a 45° angle and overlap ½".

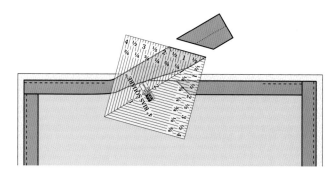

10. Join the binding ends, right sides together, using a ¼" seam allowance. (It is helpful to fold the quilt out of the way when doing this.) Press the seam open and refold the binding. Finish stitching the binding to the quilt top.

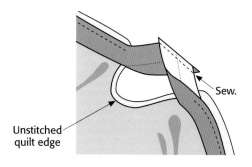

Sew.

Unstitched quilt edge

11. Trim the backing and batting ⅜" from the binding *stitching line*.

12. Gently press the right side of the binding away from the project top, using just the tip of the iron. Fold the binding to the back of the project over the raw edges, covering the machine stitching. Insert a straight pin directly into the ditch of the binding seam on the front of the project. Push the pin through all layers and bring it back up in the ditch about ½" away, being sure that the folded edge of the binding has been caught in the pin on the back of the project. Continue pinning the binding in place around the entire edge of the project. Miter the binding corners on the back of the project by forming a tuck when pinning them in place.

Quilt top

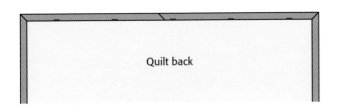

Quilt back

13. On the right side of the quilt, stitch in the ditch to secure the binding, removing the pins as the needle of the sewing machine approaches them.

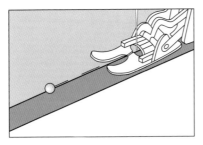

Remove pins as they approach the needle.

ATTACHING A HANGING SLEEVE

Not all the projects require a hanging sleeve, but for those that do, here are the steps:

1. Cut a piece of fabric 8" wide (less if it is a small project) and 1" shorter than the width of the project. Press the short ends under ¼" twice. Stitch close to the first folded edge.

2. Press the strip in half lengthwise, wrong sides and raw edges together. Unfold the strip and refold the long edges to meet the center crease; press the folded edges.

Center → crease

3. Open up the strip and fold it in half lengthwise, wrong sides together. Stitch the long edges together to form a tube, backstitching at the beginning and end of the seam. Center the seam in the middle of the tube and press the seam allowance open, using the tip of the iron. Be careful not to press another crease in the edges while pressing the seam open, as the previous creases will be used as stitching lines.

4. Center the fabric sleeve on the back of the project just under the binding on the top edge, with the seam allowances facing the project. Be sure the seam side of the sleeve lies flat against the backing fabric. The top side of the sleeve will have a small amount of slack in it to allow room for a hanging rod and will not lie flat. Slipstitch the sleeve in place along the creased edges of the sleeve and the bottom layer at each end. Be sure not to stitch through to the right side of the quilt.

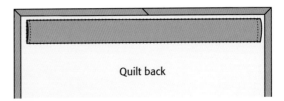

Quilt back

"WINTER" WALL HANGING

THIS SECTION CONTAINS instructions for making the blocks that compose the "Winter" wall hanging and for assembling the wall hanging itself. The blocks are arranged in order of complexity, so beginners may find it helpful to start with block 1 and progress through block 11.

You will notice that most of the appliquéd blocks are trimmed after the appliqué is applied. This is because appliqué, regardless of which application method you use, tends to draw up the background fabric to some extent. The more pieces that you appliqué to a block, the more the background tends to "shrink." Be sure to trim an even amount from all four sides so that the design remains centered.

Fabric requirements are listed for each individual block. If you plan to make the wall hanging using the same background fabric throughout, purchase a total of 2½ yards. Because some of the blocks call for cut pieces and some are paper pieced, cut all the straight-cut segments from one end of the fabric and all the paper-piecing segments from the other end to help conserve fabric.

BLOCK 1: WINTER

Finished block size: 12" x 24"

CUTTING

All measurements include ¼"-wide seam allowances.

From the white print, cut:

♦ 1 strip, 6" x 18", for background
♦ 2 strips, 3" x 42". Crosscut to make:
    2 strips, 3" x 18½", for middle top
      and bottom borders
    2 strips, 3" x 11½", for middle side borders

From the dark blue, cut:

♦ 4 strips, 1" x 42". Crosscut to make:
    2 strips, 1" x 17½", for inner top and bottom
      borders
    2 strips, 1" x 6½", for inner side borders
    2 strips, 1" x 23½", for outer top and bottom
      borders
    2 strips, 1" x 12½", for outer side borders

ASSEMBLING THE BLOCK

1. Referring to "Fusible-Web Appliqué" on pages 7–9, trace the patterns on pages 18 and 19 onto the paper side of the fusible web. Trace 1 *each* of A–F. Cut around the shapes. Fuse each shape to the wrong side of the medium blue print. Cut out the appliqués on the drawn lines and remove the paper backing. Use the patterns on pages 18 and 19 to make a placement diagram, aligning the dashed lines to make the complete diagram. Using the placement diagram, center the appliqués on the right side of the white 6" x 18" strip. Fuse in place.

2. Machine stitch around the edges of each appliqué shape, using either a buttonhole stitch, satin stitch, or zigzag stitch.

3. Trim the block to 5½" x 17½", keeping the design centered.

4. For the inner borders, stitch the dark blue 1" x 17½" strips to the top and bottom edges of the quilt block. Press the seams toward the border strips. Stitch the dark blue 1" x 6½" strips to the sides of the quilt block. Press the seams toward the border strips.

    For the middle borders, stitch the white 3" x 18½" strips to the top and bottom edges of the quilt block. Press the seams toward the borders. Stitch the white 3" x 11½" strips to the sides of the quilt block. Press the seams toward the borders.

    For the outer borders, stitch the dark blue 1" x 23½" strips to the top and bottom edges of the quilt block. Press the seams toward the borders. Stitch the dark blue 1" x 12½" strips to the sides of the quilt block. Press the seams toward the borders.

Block 1: Winter
Appliqué Patterns

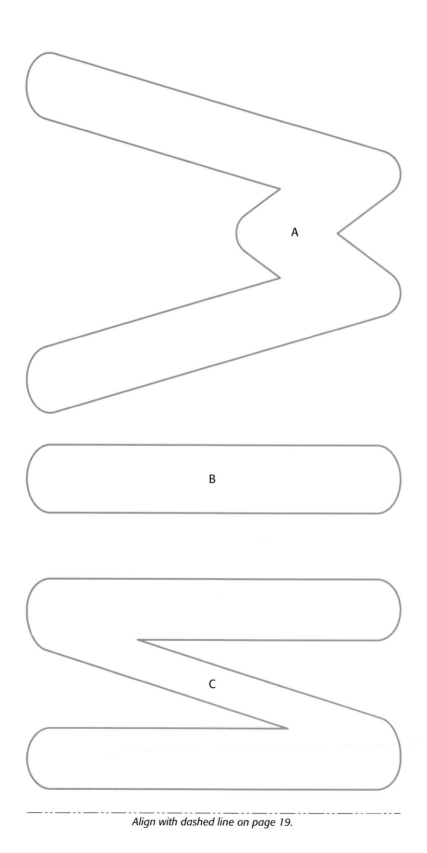

A

B

C

Align with dashed line on page 19.

Block 1: Winter
Appliqué Patterns

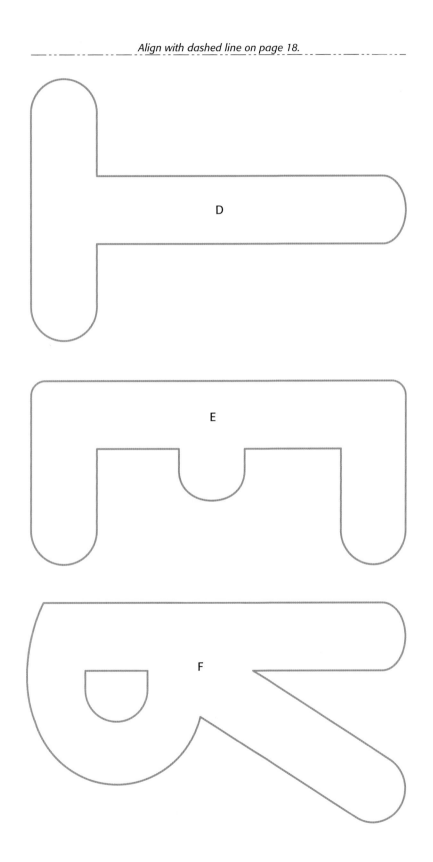

Align with dashed line on page 18.

D

E

F

BLOCK 2: EVERGREEN TREE

Finished block size: 3" x 12"

MATERIALS

Yardage is based on 42"-wide fabric.
Materials listed are enough to make 2 blocks.

- ✦ ⅛ yard of white print for background
- ✦ Scraps of 3 assorted greens for tree sections
- ✦ Scrap of dark brown for tree trunks
- ✦ Foundation paper

ASSEMBLING THE BLOCKS

1. Referring to "Paper Piecing" on pages 10 and 11, copy or trace the foundation patterns on page 21 onto foundation paper. Make 2 patterns of each unit. Paper piece each unit, referring to the patterns for the appropriate fabric to use in each section of each unit.

2. After all the pieces have been added, trim only the edges of each unit that will be joined to another unit. Stitch each A unit to a B unit. Press the seams toward unit A. Stitch a C unit to each A-B unit. Press the seams toward unit C. Remove the paper from the seam allowances only. Turn the blocks to the paper side. Trim each block to 3½" x 12½" along the outside dotted lines. Do not remove the paper foundation until the blocks are set into the project. This will eliminate any stretching that can occur when the bias edges are handled.

Block 2: Evergreen Tree
Foundation Patterns

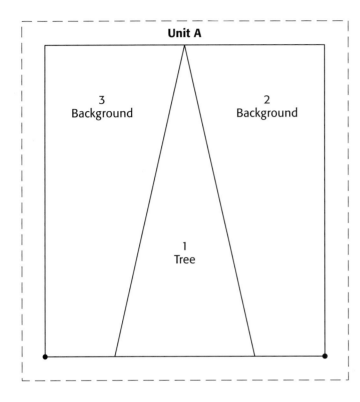

Unit A

3
Background

2
Background

1
Tree

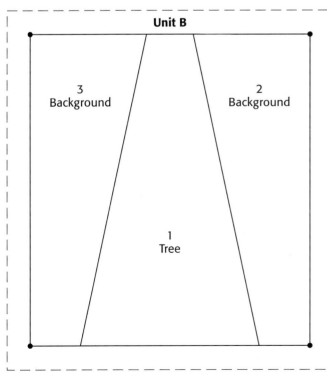

Unit B

3
Background

2
Background

1
Tree

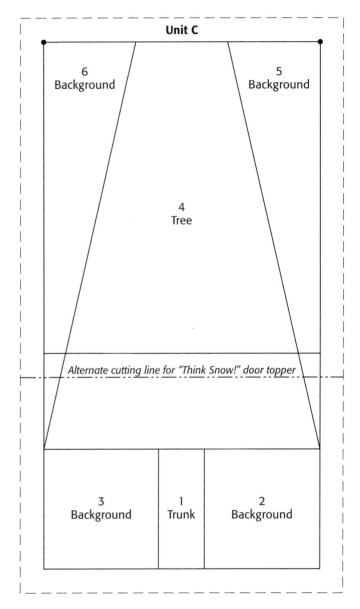

Unit C

6
Background

5
Background

4
Tree

Alternate cutting line for "Think Snow!" door topper

3
Background

1
Trunk

2
Background

BLOCK 3: SLED

Finished block size: 9" x 12"

MATERIALS

Yardage is based on 42"-wide fabric.

♦ 10" x 13" rectangle of white print for background
♦ 7" x 8" rectangle of red barn board print for sled
♦ 5" x 6" rectangle of black for sled rails
♦ 10" x 10" square of paper-backed fusible web
♦ Appliqué pressing sheet

ASSEMBLING THE BLOCK

1. Referring to "Fusible-Web Appliqué" on pages 7–9, trace the appliqué patterns on page 23 onto the paper side of the fusible web. Trace 2 *each* of D, E, and H, and 1 *each* of the remaining pieces. Cut around the shapes. Fuse each appliqué shape onto the wrong side of the appropriate fabric. Cut out the appliqués on the drawn lines and remove the paper backing. Because the sled is a symmetrical design, there is no need to reverse it to make the placement diagram. Simply trace the appliqué pattern as drawn. Using an appliqué pressing sheet and the placement diagram, fuse the appliqué shapes together.

2. Center the appliqué unit on the right side of the background rectangle; fuse it in place.

3. Machine stitch around the edges of each appliqué shape, using either a buttonhole stitch, satin stitch, or zigzag stitch.

4. Trim the block to 9½" x 12½", keeping the design centered.

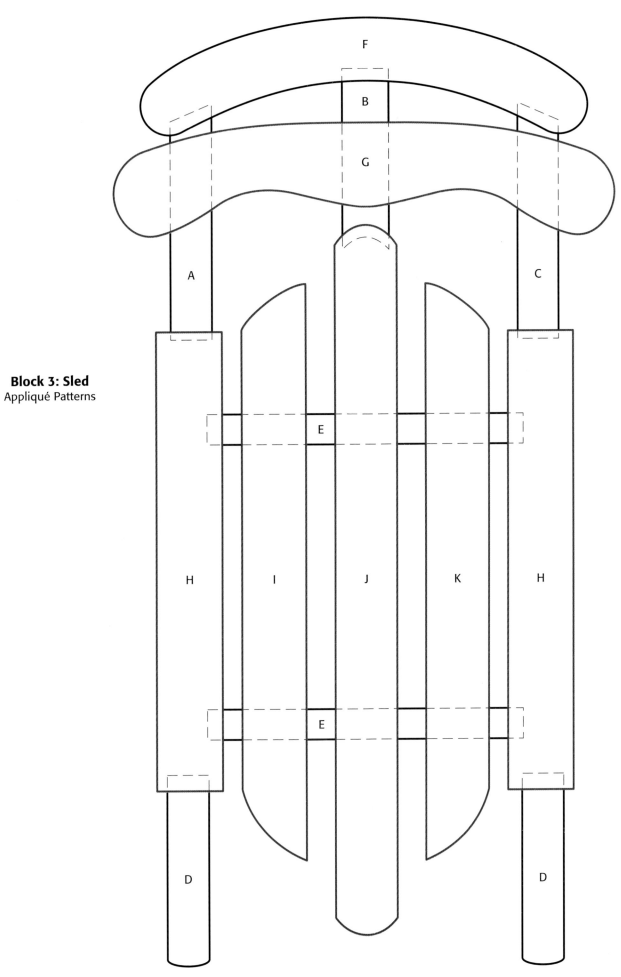

Block 3: Sled
Appliqué Patterns

BLOCK 4: HOLLY LEAVES

Finished block size: 6" x 6"

CUTTING

All measurements include ¼"-wide seam allowances.

From *each* of the 6 assorted greens, cut:
+ 1 strip, 1½" x 7", for leaves

MATERIALS

Yardage is based on 42"-wide fabric.
Materials listed are enough to make 2 blocks.

+ 2 squares, 7" x 7", of light blue for background
+ ⅛ yard *total* of 6 assorted greens for leaves
+ 9" x 9" square of paper-backed fusible web
+ 6 red ½"-diameter buttons for holly berries

ASSEMBLING THE BLOCKS

1. With right sides together, sew 2 green 1½" x 7" strips together along the long edges. Trim the seam to ⅛" and press open. Make 3.

2. Referring to "Fusible-Web Appliqué" on pages 7–9, trace the appliqué pattern on page 25 onto the paper side of the fusible web. Trace 6. Be sure to trace the center line onto the leaf shapes. Cut around the shapes. Fuse 2 leaf appliqué shapes onto the wrong side of each pieced leaf strip from step 1, aligning the appliqué-shape center line with the fabric seam line. Cut out the appliqués on the outside drawn line and remove the paper backing.

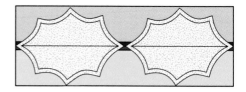

3. Position 3 of the leaves on the right side of a background square as shown, leaving an equal amount of space between the tip of each leaf and the block outer edge. Fuse in place. Make 2.

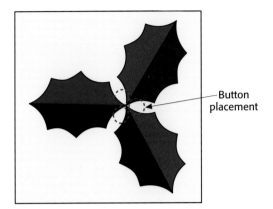

Button placement

4. Machine stitch around the edges of each appliqué shape, using either a buttonhole stitch, satin stitch, or zigzag stitch.

5. Trim each block to 6½" x 6½", keeping the design centered.

6. After the wall hanging is completed, stitch 3 red buttons to each block where indicated for berries.

Block 4: Holly Leaves
Appliqué Pattern

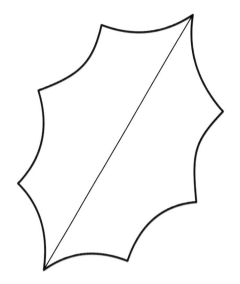

BLOCK 5: ICE SKATES

Finished block size: 6" x 12"

ASSEMBLING THE BLOCK

1. Referring to "Fusible-Web Appliqué" on pages 7–9, trace the appliqué patterns on page 27 onto the paper side of the fusible web. Trace 2 *each* of A–C. Cut around the shapes. Fuse each appliqué shape onto the wrong side of the appropriate fabric. Cut out the appliqués on the drawn lines and remove the paper backing. Using the patterns on page 27, make a placement diagram. Using an appliqué pressing sheet and the placement diagram, fuse the appliqué shapes together. Make 2.

2. Position the appliqués on the background rectangle as shown. Fuse the appliqués in place.

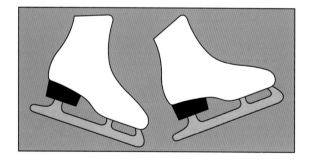

3. Mark the stitching detail lines on the ice skates for laces.

MATERIALS

Yardage is based on 42"-wide fabric.

- ✦ 7" x 13" rectangle of medium blue for background
- ✦ 7" x 7" square of white for skates
- ✦ 2" x 3" rectangle of black for heels
- ✦ 3" x 6" rectangle of gray for blades
- ✦ 6" x 12" rectangle of paper-backed fusible web
- ✦ Appliqué pressing sheet
- ✦ Black embroidery thread for soles
- ✦ 1 yard of ⅛"-wide white double-faced satin ribbon

4. Machine stitch around the edges of each appliqué shape, using either a buttonhole stitch, satin stitch, or zigzag stitch. To make the soles of the ice skates, machine satin stitch along the bottom of each shoe, using black embroidery thread. Satin stitch over the lace detail lines using a narrow satin stitch and white thread.

5. Trim the block to 6½" x 12½", keeping the design centered.

6. Cut the ribbon into 2 equal lengths. Make a small bow at the center of each length. After the wall hanging is completed, tack one of the bows to each skate where indicated, and trim the excess ribbon as desired. Be sure to sew through the knot. This will secure the ribbon and prevent the bow from coming untied. The ribbon tails also may be tacked to the wall hanging to keep them in place.

Block 5: Ice Skates
Appliqué Patterns

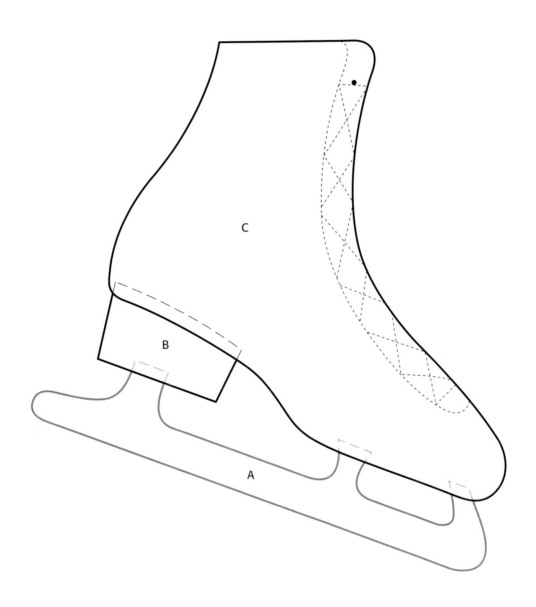

BLOCK 6: PATCHWORK MITTEN

Finished block size: 6" x 6"

ASSEMBLING THE BLOCKS

1. Referring to "Paper Piecing" on pages 10 and 11, use the pattern on page 29 to copy or trace 1 mitten foundation pattern and 1 reverse mitten foundation pattern. Paper piece the foundation units using the 5 coordinating blue fabrics; trim the seams to ⅛" after each addition. After adding all the pieces, trim the foundation squares along the pattern outer edges and remove the paper from the back of the blocks.

2. Referring to "Fusible-Web Appliqué" on pages 7–9, use the appliqué pattern on page 30 to trace 1 mitten and 1 reverse mitten onto the paper side of the fusible web. Be sure to trace the inner lines onto the mittens. Cut around the shapes.

3. Place a foundation-pieced square on the ironing board, wrong side up. Position a fusible-web mitten on the square, aligning the lines on the shape with the fabric seams. Fuse the shape in place. Repeat with the remaining foundation square and mitten shape.

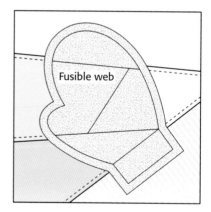

Align traced lines over
foundation seam lines.

4. Cut out the appliqués on the outer drawn lines and remove the paper backing.

5. Center each appliqué on the right side of a background square; fuse in place.

6. With a decorative machine stitch and contrasting

thread, stitch over the seams of each mitten if desired. Machine stitch around the edges of the appliqué shapes, using either a buttonhole stitch, satin stitch, or zigzag stitch.

7. Trim each block to 6½" x 6½", keeping the design centered.

Block 6: Patchwork Mitten
Foundation Pattern

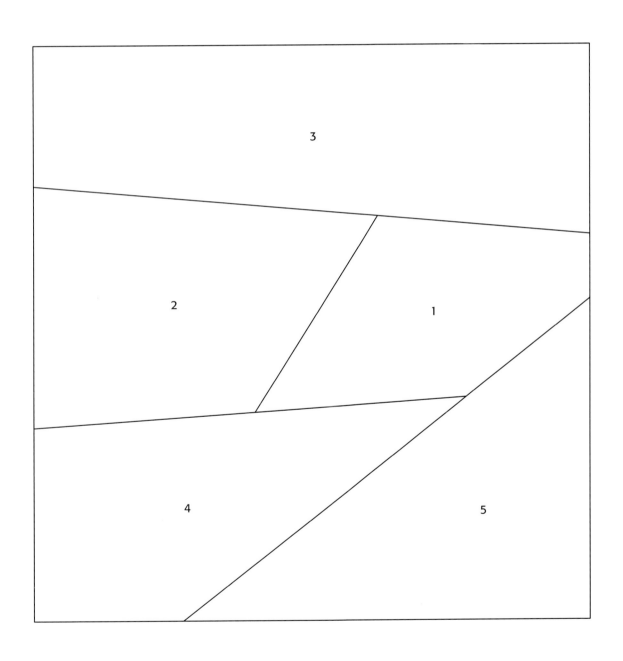

Block 6: Patchwork Mitten
Appliqué Pattern

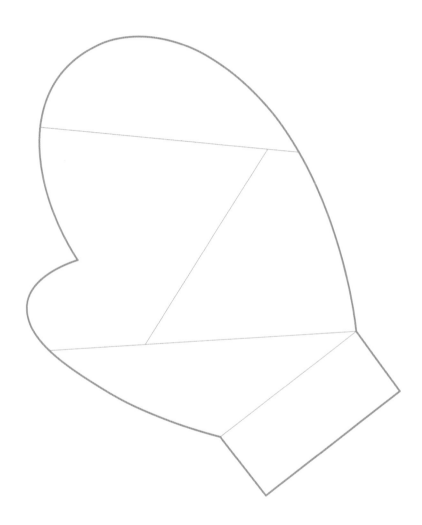

BLOCK 7: BIRDHOUSE

Finished block size: 9" x 9"

ASSEMBLING THE BLOCK

1. Referring to "Paper Piecing" on pages 10 and 11, copy or trace the foundation patterns on pages 32 and 33 onto foundation paper. Paper piece each unit, referring to the pattern for the appropriate fabric to use in each section of each unit.

2. After all the pieces have been added, trim only the edges of each unit that will be joined to another unit. Stitch the units together. Remove the paper from the seam allowances only. Press the seam toward unit B. Turn the block to the paper side. Trim the block to 9½" x 9½" along the outside dotted lines. Carefully remove the paper foundation.

NOTE: *Because appliqué pieces will be added to this block, the paper must be removed before the block is set into the quilt. Handle the block carefully so as not to distort any bias edges.*

MATERIALS

Yardage is based on 42"-wide fabric.

- ¼ yard of light blue snow print for background
- 7" x 7" square of wood print #1 for birdhouse
- 6" x 8" rectangle of white for snow
- Scrap of black for hole
- Scrap of wood print #2 for pole and perch
- Foundation paper
- 6" x 8" rectangle of paper-backed fusible web

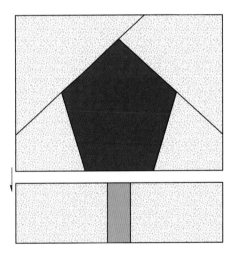

3. Referring to "Fusible-Web Appliqué" on pages 7–9, trace the appliqué patterns on page 33 onto the paper side of the fusible web. Trace 1 *each* of A–F. Cut around the shapes. Fuse each appliqué shape onto the wrong side of the appropriate fabric. Cut out the appliqués on the drawn lines and remove the paper backing. Using the placement lines on the foundation pattern and the photo above left as a guide, fuse the appliqué shapes in place.

4. Machine stitch around the edges of each appliqué, using either a buttonhole stitch, satin stitch, or zigzag stitch.

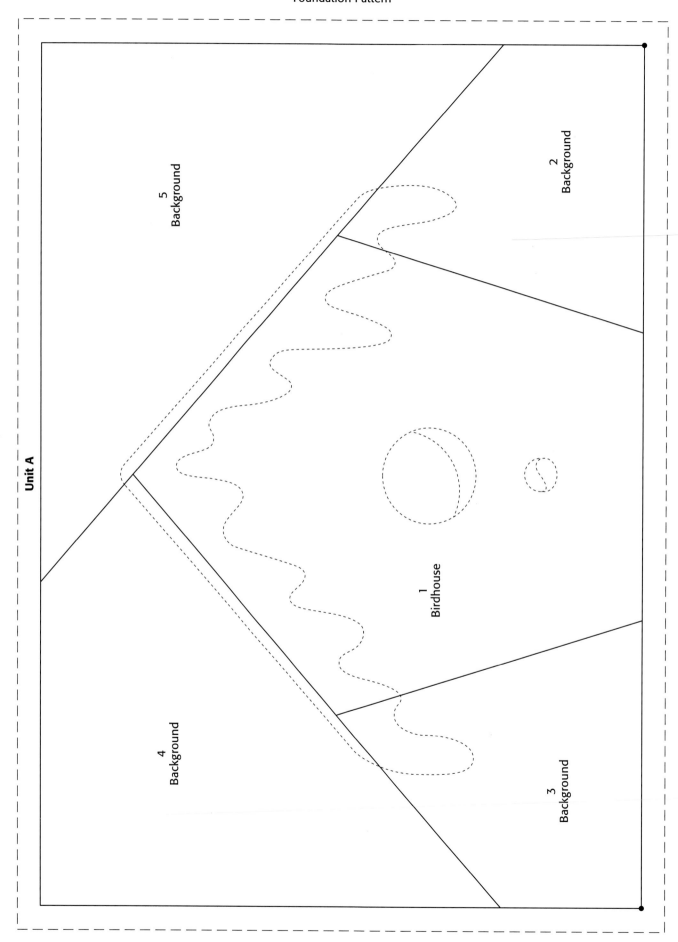

Unit A

5
Background

2
Background

1
Birdhouse

4
Background

3
Background

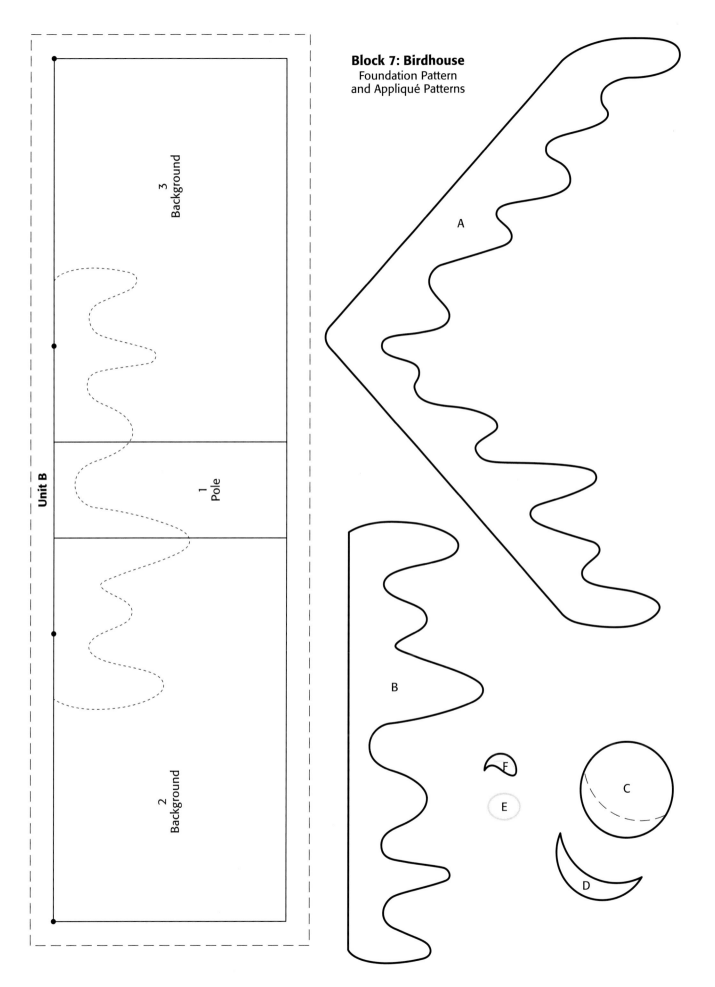

Block 7: Birdhouse
Foundation Pattern
and Appliqué Patterns

Unit B

3
Background

1
Pole

2
Background

A

B

C

D

E

F

BLOCK 8: WINTER CABIN

Finished block size: 9" x 12"

CUTTING

All measurements include ¼"-wide seam allowances.

From the light blue snow print, cut:
+ 2 strips, 3½" x 8¼", for sides of cabin

From the white, cut:
+ 1 strip, 1¾" x 12½", for bottom of cabin

ASSEMBLING THE BLOCK

1. Referring to "Paper Piecing" on pages 10 and 11, copy or trace the foundation patterns on page 36 onto foundation paper. Paper piece each unit, referring to the pattern for the appropriate fabric to use in each section of each unit.

2. After all the pieces have been added, trim only the edges of each unit that will be joined to another unit. Stitch the units together and remove the paper from the seam allowances only. Press the seam toward unit A. Turn the block to the paper side. Trim the block to 6½" x 8¼" along the outside dotted lines.

MATERIALS

Yardage is based on 42"-wide fabric.

+ ¼ yard of light blue snow print for background
+ ¼ yard of wood print for cabin
+ ¼ yard of white for snow
+ Scrap of dark green for cabin door
+ Scrap of pale yellow for cabin window
+ Scrap of brick print for chimney
+ 5" x 9" rectangle of paper-backed fusible web

NOTE: *If you are using directional fabrics for the cabin (for example, wood planks), be sure the fabric is oriented in the correct direction before you cut.*

3. Stitch the light blue snow-print 3½" x 8¼" strips to each side of the foundation-pieced cabin as shown. Press the seams toward the strips. Stitch the white 1¾" x 12½" strip to the bottom of the pieced unit as shown. Press the seam toward the white strip.

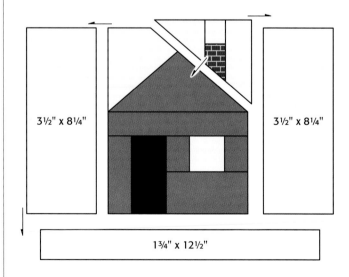

4. Referring to "Fusible-Web Appliqué" on pages 7–9, trace the appliqué patterns below onto the paper side of the fusible web. Trace 1 *each* of A and B. Cut around the shapes. Fuse each appliqué shape onto the wrong side of the white fabric. Cut out the appliqués on the drawn lines and remove the paper backing. Using the placement lines on the foundation pattern and the photo on page 34 as a guide, fuse the appliqué shapes in place.

5. Machine stitch around the edges of each appliqué shape, using either a buttonhole stitch, satin stitch, or zigzag stitch.

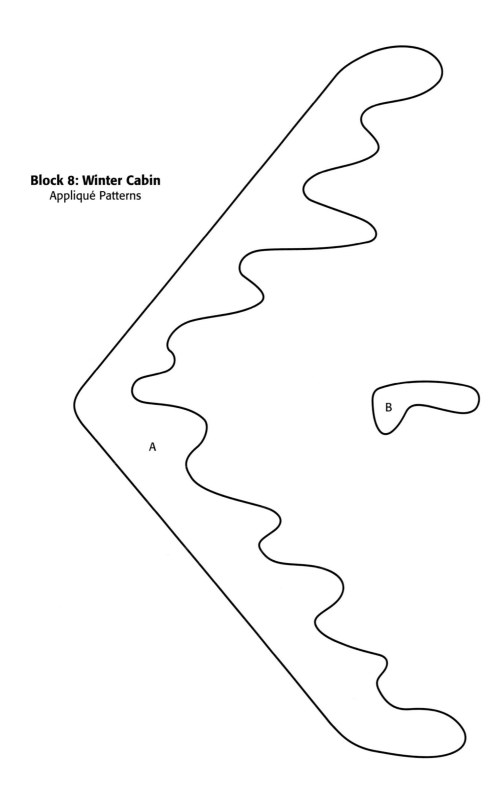

Block 8: Winter Cabin
Appliqué Patterns

Block 8: Winter Cabin
Foundation Patterns

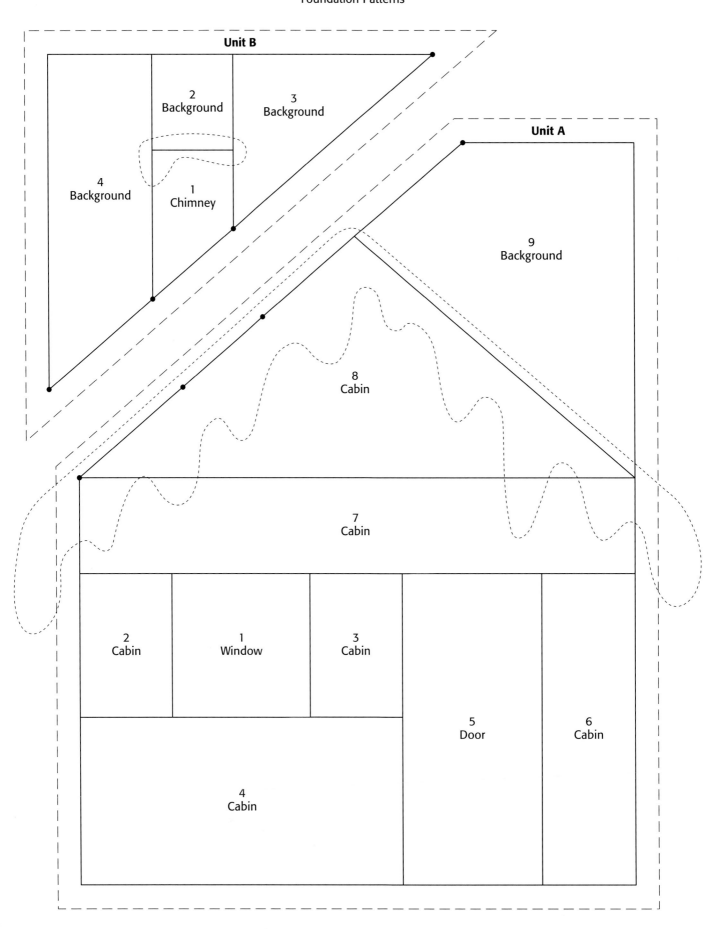

BLOCK 9: SNOWMAN

Finished block size: 9" x 12"

MATERIALS

Yardage is based on 42"-wide fabric.

✦ 10" x 11¾" rectangle of light blue for background top
✦ 7" x 10" rectangle of white #1 for snowman body
✦ 1¾" x 10" rectangle of white #2 for background bottom
✦ 5" x 5" square of green print for vest
✦ 5" x 5" square of multicolored print for scarf and hat border
✦ 3" x 4" rectangle of off-white for sign
✦ 1" x 5" rectangle of wood print for signpost
✦ Scrap of red-on-red stripe for hat
✦ Scrap of red print suitable for pom-pom
✦ Scrap of orange for nose
✦ 11" x 11" square of paper-backed fusible web
✦ Appliqué pressing sheet
✦ Black permanent-ink fabric marker
✦ 6 black ⅛"-diameter buttons for eyes and mouth

ASSEMBLING THE BLOCK

1. With right sides together, sew the white and light blue background rectangles together along the 10" edges. Press the seam open.

2. Referring to "Fusible-Web Appliqué" on pages 7–9, trace the appliqué patterns on page 39 onto the paper side of the fusible web. Trace 1 *each* of A–N. Cut around the shapes, removing fusible web inside the larger shapes, if desired. Fuse each appliqué shape to the wrong side of the appropriate fabric. Cut out the appliqués on the drawn lines and remove the paper backing. Use the pattern on page 39 to make a placement diagram. Place the sign appliqué (F) over the placement diagram and trace

the lettering onto the fabric with the marker. Using an appliqué pressing sheet and the placement diagram, fuse the appliqué shapes together.

3. Place the appliqué unit on the background rectangle, positioning the snowman body so that the bottom of the sides are flush with the background seam and the center of the body extends into the white rectangle. Fuse in place.

1¼"

Place bottom of snowman on seam line.

4. Mark the stitching detail line on the snowman vest; satin stitch.

5. Machine stitch around the edges of each appliqué shape, using either a buttonhole stitch, satin stitch, or zigzag stitch.

6. Trim the block to 9½" x 12½", keeping the design centered and aligning the background seam 1¼" from the bottom of the block.

7. After the project is completed, stitch the buttons to the snowman's head where indicated for eyes and mouth.

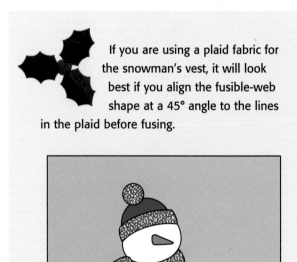

If you are using a plaid fabric for the snowman's vest, it will look best if you align the fusible-web shape at a 45° angle to the lines in the plaid before fusing.

Block 9: Snowman
Appliqué Patterns

Button placement

Think
Snow!

BLOCK 10: CARDINAL

Finished block size: 9" x 9"

ASSEMBLING THE BLOCK

1. Referring to "Paper Piecing" on pages 10 and 11, copy or trace the foundation patterns on pages 41–44 onto foundation paper. Paper piece each unit, referring to the pattern for the appropriate fabric to use in each section of each unit.

2. After all the pieces have been added, trim only the edges of each unit that will be joined to another unit. Stitch the units together in the order shown at right. When all the units have been joined, remove the paper from the seam allowances only. Press the seams in whichever direction they naturally turn. Turn the block to the paper side. Trim the block to 9½" x 9½". Carefully remove the paper foundation.

   NOTE: *Because appliqué pieces will be added to this block, the paper must be removed before the block is set into the quilt. Handle the block carefully so as not to distort any bias edges.*

MATERIALS

Yardage is based on 42"-wide fabric.

- ✦ ¼ yard of white print for background
- ✦ 1½" x 3½" strip *each* of 4 assorted greens for holly leaves
- ✦ Scrap of bright red for cardinal head and breast
- ✦ Scrap of dark red for cardinal tail and wings
- ✦ Scrap of black for cardinal mask
- ✦ Scrap of gold for cardinal beak
- ✦ Scrap of brown for branch
- ✦ Foundation paper
- ✦ 4" x 6" rectangle of paper-backed fusible web
- ✦ 1 black ³⁄₁₆"-diameter button for cardinal eye
- ✦ 1 red ³⁄₈"-diameter button for holly berry

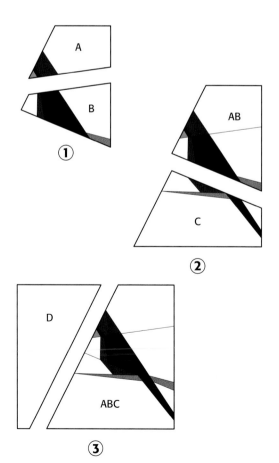

3. With right sides together, sew 2 green 1½" x 3½" strips together along the long edges. Trim the seam to ⅛" and press open. Make 2.

4. Referring to "Fusible-Web Appliqué" on pages 7–9, trace 2 holly-leaf appliqué patterns on page 25 onto the paper side of the fusible web. Be sure to trace the center line onto each leaf shape. Cut around the shapes. Fuse 1 leaf appliqué shape to the wrong side of each pieced leaf strip from step 3, aligning the appliqué-shape center line with the fabric seam line. Cut out the appliqués on the drawn lines and remove the paper backing.

5. Referring to the photo as a guide, arrange the leaves on the cardinal block; fuse in place.

6. Machine stitch around each appliqué shape, using either a buttonhole stitch, satin stitch, or zigzag stitch.

7. After the project is completed, stitch the black button to the bird's head where indicated for the eye and the red button between the leaves for the holly berry.

Block 10: Cardinal
Foundation Pattern

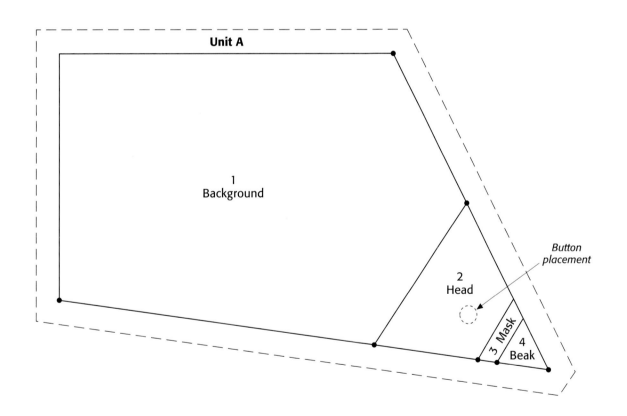

Block 10: Cardinal
Foundation Pattern

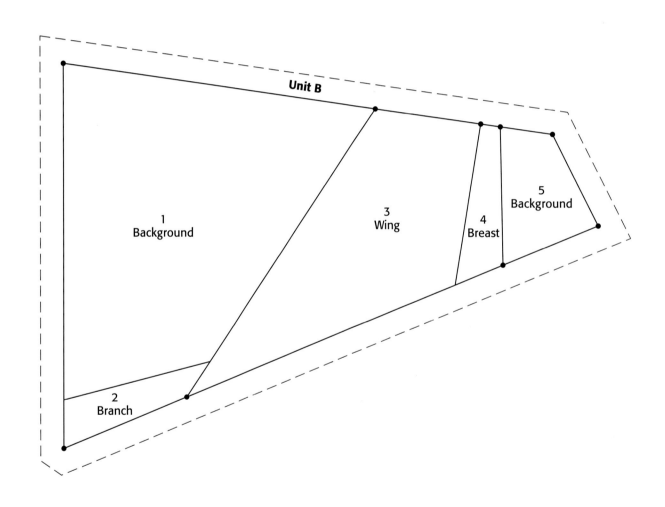

Unit B

1
Background

2
Branch

3
Wing

4
Breast

5
Background

Block 10: Cardinal
Foundation Pattern

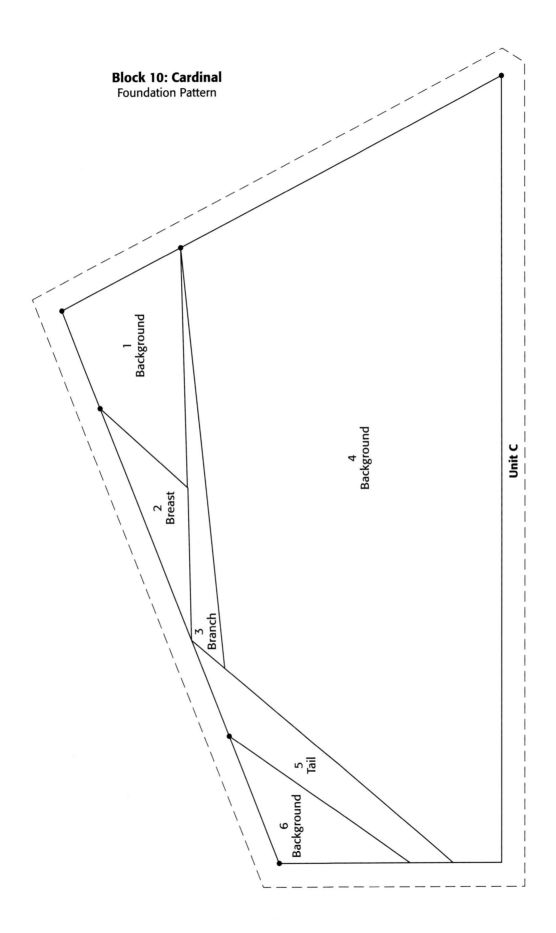

1
Background

2
Breast

3
Branch

4
Background

5
Tail

6
Background

Unit C

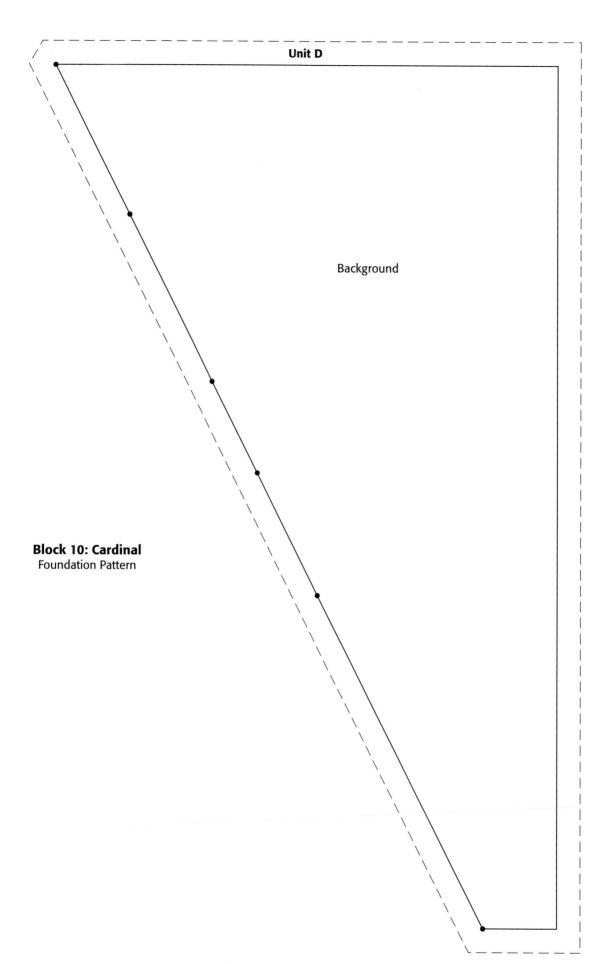

Unit D

Background

Block 10: Cardinal
Foundation Pattern

BLOCK 11: SNOWFLAKE

Finished block size: 6" x 6"

CUTTING

All measurements include ¼"-wide seam allowances.

From the white print, cut:

✦ 4 squares, 7" x 7", for background

ASSEMBLING THE BLOCKS

1. Referring to "Fusible-Web Appliqué" on pages 7–9, trace the appliqué pattern on page 46 onto the paper side of the fusible web. Trace 6. Cut around the shapes. Fuse 2 appliqué shapes to the wrong side of the remaining white print. Fuse 4 appliqué shapes to the wrong side of the medium blue #1 fabric. Cut out the appliqués on the drawn lines and remove the paper backing. Be sure to cut out the 6 diamond shapes inside of the snowflakes. Center the white appliqué shapes on the right side of the light blue and medium blue #2 background squares and fuse in place. Center the blue appliqué shapes on the right side of the white background squares and fuse in place.

> ## MATERIALS
> *Yardage is based on 42"-wide fabric.*
> *Materials listed are enough to make 6 blocks.*
>
> ✦ ¼ yard of white print for background and snowflakes
> ✦ 12" x 12" square of medium blue #1 for snowflakes
> ✦ 7" x 7" square of light blue for background
> ✦ 7" x 7" square of medium blue #2 for background
> ✦ 12" x 18" rectangle of paper-backed fusible web

2. Machine stitch around the edges of each appliqué shape, using either a buttonhole stitch, satin stitch, or zigzag stitch.

3. Trim each block to 6½" x 6½", keeping the design centered.

Block 11: Snowflake
Appliqué Pattern

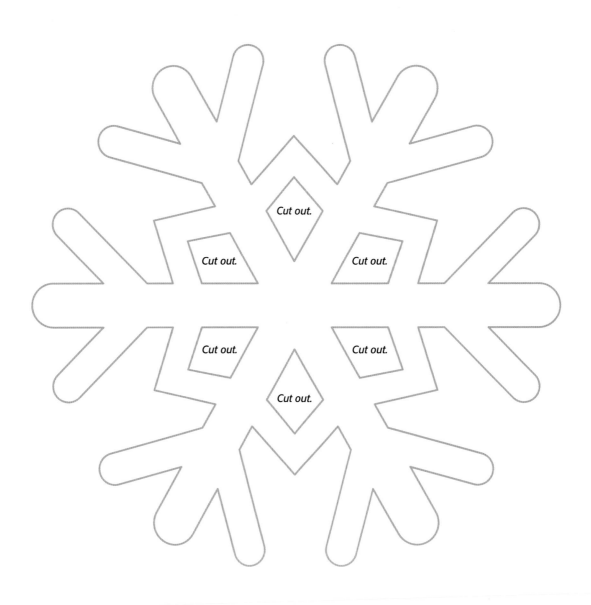

Cut out.

Cut out.

Cut out.

Cut out.

Cut out.

Cut out.

FRIENDSHIP STAR BLOCKS

Finished block size: 3" x 3"

CUTTING

All measurements include ¼"-wide seam allowances.

From the assorted medium and dark blues, cut 18 sets of the following:

- ♦ 4 squares, 1½" x 1½", for corner squares
- ♦ 2 squares, 1⅞" x 1⅞"; cut each square in half diagonally to make 4 half-square triangles for star points

From the white print, cut:

- ♦ 18 squares, 1½" x 1½", for star centers
- ♦ 36 squares, 1⅞" x 1⅞"; cut each square in half diagonally to make 72 half-square triangles for star points

ASSEMBLING THE BLOCKS

1. With right sides together, stitch each blue triangle to a white triangle along the long edges to form a square. Press the seams toward the blue triangles. Trim the points. Make 72 half-square-triangle units.

Make 72.

MATERIALS

Yardage is based on 42"-wide fabric.
Materials listed are enough to make 18 blocks.

- ♦ ⅜ yard *total* of assorted medium and dark blues for star backgrounds
- ♦ ¼ yard of white print for stars

2. Stitch 4 blue squares, 4 half-square-triangle units from step 1, and 1 white square together as shown. Make sure the blue fabric in each unit of the block is the same. Press the seams in the directions indicated. Make 18.

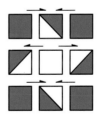 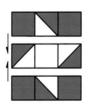

Make 18.

WALL-HANGING CONSTRUCTION

Finished wall-hanging size: 51" x 51"

CUTTING

All measurements include ¼"-wide seam allowances.

From the medium blue, cut:
- ✦ 4 strips, 1½" x 42". Crosscut to make:
    2 strips, 1½" x 36½", for inner side borders
    2 strips, 1½" x 38½", for inner top and bottom borders
- ✦ 6 strips, 2½" x 42", for binding

From the white print, cut:
- ✦ 3 strips, 6¾" x 42", for outer-border triangles

From the blue print, cut:
- ✦ 2 strips, 6¾" x 42", for outer-border triangles
- ✦ 4 rectangles, 5½" x 7", for outer-border end triangles

From the backing, cut:
- ✦ 2 rectangles, 42" x 54"

From the batting, cut:
- ✦ 1 square, 54" x 54"

ASSEMBLING THE WALL-HANGING TOP

1. Referring to the block instructions on pages 17–47, make 1 *each* of blocks 1, 3, 5, and 7–10. Make 2 *each* of blocks 2, 4, and 6. Make 6 of block 11. Refer to page 47 to make 18 Friendship Star blocks. The materials listed for each block will make the required number.

2. Sew the Friendship Star blocks into strips as shown. Make 3 strips of 4 Friendship Star blocks and 2 strips of 3 Friendship Star blocks.

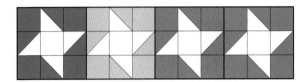

Make 3.

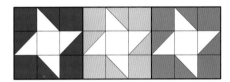

Make 2.

3. Arrange the blocks and Friendship Star strips into 3 horizontal rows as shown. Stitch the blocks and Friendship Star strips in each row in the order shown. Press the seam allowances in the direction shown. Stitch the rows together.

4. For the inner border, stitch the medium blue 1½" x 36½" strips to the wall-hanging sides. Press the seams toward the strips. Stitch the medium blue 1½" x 38½" strips to the top and bottom edges of the wall hanging. Press the seams toward the strips.

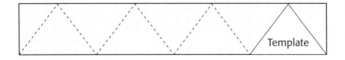

5. To make the outer-border strips, trace the template pattern on page 51 onto heavy cardboard or template plastic and cut out on the drawn line. Stack the 3 white strips on top of each other so that all the edges are aligned. Working on a flat cutting surface, place the long edge of the template along the long edge of the fabric strips. Cut the first set of 3 triangles. Rotate the template 180° and cut the next set of 3 triangles. Repeat this procedure to cut 16 white background triangles. Repeat the procedure with the blue 6¾" x 42" strips to cut 12 triangles.

6. Place 2 blue 5½" x 7" rectangles right sides together. Cut in half diagonally from corner to corner. Repeat with the remaining rectangles to make 8 outside-border end triangles.

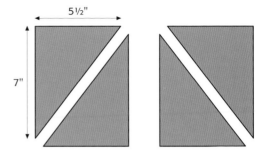

7. Beginning and ending with a white background border triangle, alternately stitch 4 background triangles and 3 blue triangles together. Stitch an end triangle to each end of the strip. Make 4.

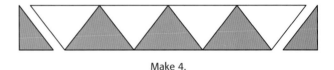

Make 4.

8. Sew an outer-border strip to the top and bottom edges of the quilt top, placing the blue fabric next to the inner border. Press the seams toward the inner border. Stitch 1 block 11 to each end of the remaining border strips as shown. Stitch the border strips to the sides of the quilt top. Press the seams toward the inner border.

FINISHING THE WALL HANGING

1. Refer to "Project Finishing" on pages 12–15 to layer, quilt, and bind the wall hanging.

2. Sew the buttons to the holly leaves (blocks 4 and 10) for berries, the snowman (block 9) for mouth and eyes, and the cardinal (block 10) for the bird's eye where indicated. Sew the ribbon bows to the ice skates (block 5) for laces.

3. Sew a hanging sleeve to the back of the quilt.

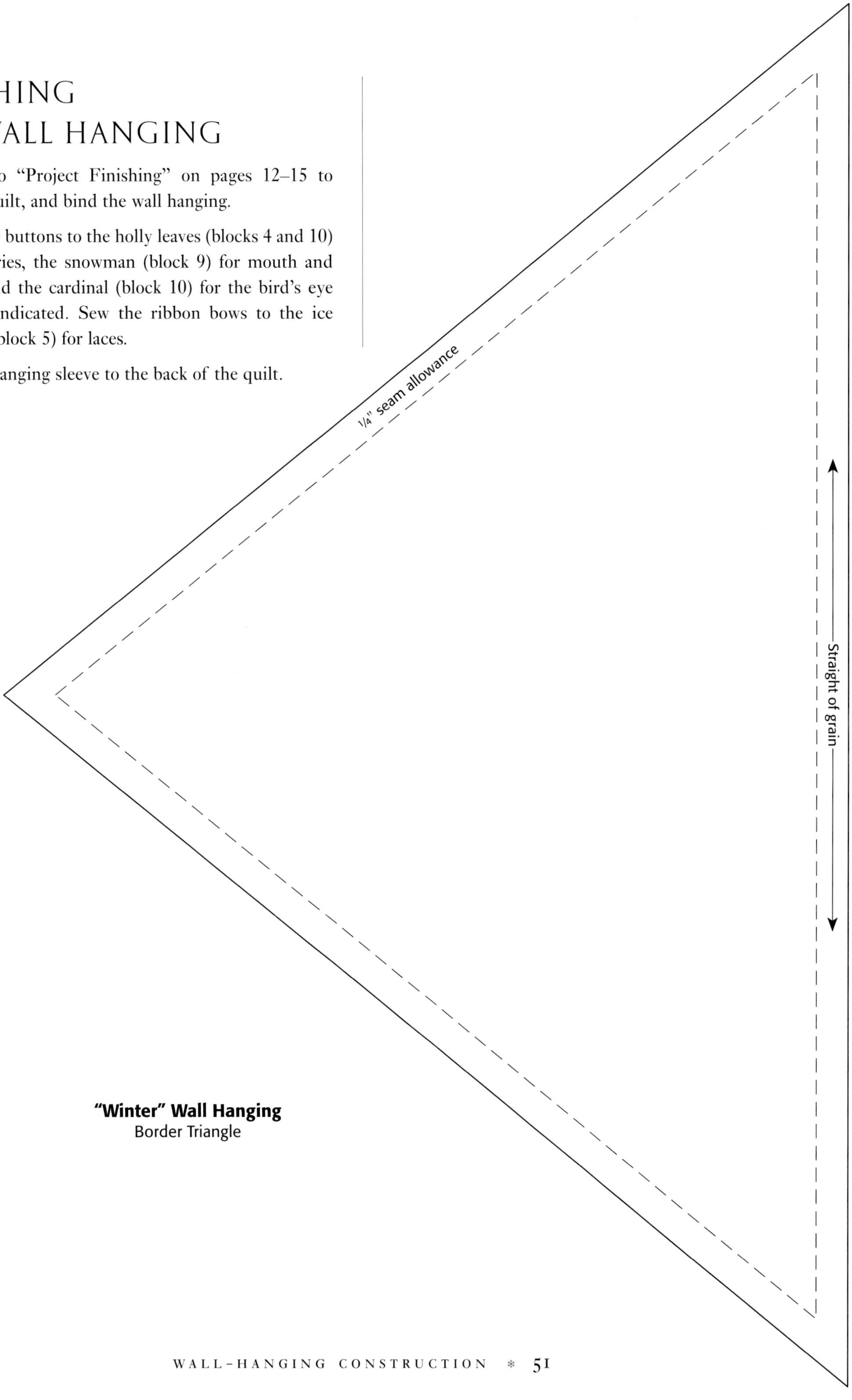

¼" seam allowance

Straight of grain

"Winter" Wall Hanging
Border Triangle

"WINTER" MANTEL BANNER

Finished mantel-banner size: 35" wide

CUTTING

All measurements include ¼"-wide seam allowances.

From the blue snowflake print, cut:
- ◆ 3 strips, 5½" x 42". Crosscut to make:
  2 strips, 5½" x 11½", for appliqué backgrounds
  2 strips, 5½" x 14½", for appliqué backgrounds
  2 strips, 5½" x 17½", for appliqué backgrounds
- ◆ 1 strip, mantel depth* x 35½", for mantel piece

From the coordinating print, cut:
- ◆ 3 strips, 5½" x 42". Crosscut to make:
  2 strips, 5½" x 11½", for backing
  2 strips, 5½" x 14½", for backing
  2 strips, 5½" x 17½", for backing
- ◆ 1 strip, mantel depth* x 35½", for backing

From the batting, cut:
- ◆ 2 strips, 5½" x 11½"
- ◆ 2 strips, 5½" x 14½"
- ◆ 2 strips, 5½" x 17½"

Measure the depth of the fireplace mantel (from the back wall to the front edge of the mantel) on which the banner will hang. Add ½" to this measurement.

ASSEMBLING THE BANNER

1. Fold one of the 5½"-wide blue snowflake-print pieces in half lengthwise, right sides together. Using the 6" Bias Square ruler, place the 45° line on the ruler along the fold of the rectangle, with the corner of the ruler at the folded point of the piece as shown. Trim the outer corners away from the rectangle, creating a point. Repeat with the remaining background, backing, and batting pieces.

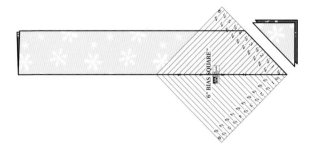

2. Referring to "Fusible-Web Appliqué" on pages 7–9, trace the winter appliqué patterns on pages 18 and 19 onto the paper side of the fusible web. Trace one each of A–F. Cut around the shapes. Fuse each appliqué shape to the wrong side of the silver print. Cut out the appliqués on the drawn lines and remove the paper backing.

3. Position the appliqué shapes on the right side of the appropriate blue snowflake-print pieces, centering each letter 2½" from the point of the banner. Place the "W" and "R" appliqués on the 5½" x 17½" strips, the "I" and "E" appliqués on the 5½" x 14½" strips, and the "N" and "T" appliqués on the 5½" x 11½" strips. Fuse in place.

4. Machine stitch around the edges of each appliqué shape, using a buttonhole stitch, satin stitch, or zigzag stitch.

5. Place one of the batting rectangles on a flat surface. Place an appliquéd piece of the same dimension on top of the batting, right side up. Place a backing piece of the same dimension on top of the appliquéd piece, wrong side up. Smooth out any wrinkles, and pin all 3 layers together. Using a walking foot and a

¼" seam allowance, stitch along both long edges and the pointed end, leaving the straight end open. Backstitch at the beginning and end of the stitching line. Repeat with the remaining 5 appliquéd pieces. Trim the points and turn right side out. Using a point turner, carefully push out the corners of each appliquéd unit. Lightly press the edges of each unit so that they lie flat.

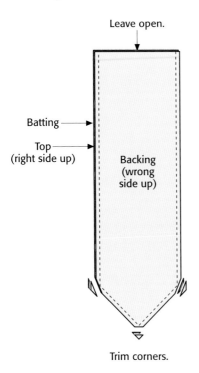

Leave open.

Batting

Top
(right side up)

Backing
(wrong
side up)

Trim corners.

6. Topstitch ¼" from the sides and pointed end of each appliquéd piece. Quilt each piece if desired.

7. Fold the remaining background strip in half width-wise and finger-press along the fold line to mark the center point. Open up the strip and place a pin on one edge at the fold line. Place the strip on a flat surface, right side up. Pin each appliquéd piece in place as shown so the finished banner will spell "WINTER." Machine baste the appliquéd pieces in place along the short ends, using a scant ¼" seam allowance.

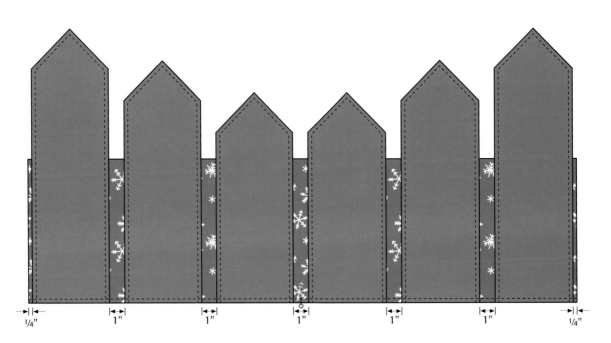

¼"   1"   1"   1"   1"   1"   ¼"

8. Pin back each appliquéd piece so it will not get caught in the seam allowance. Place the remaining backing strip over the mantel-banner top, wrong side up. Pin in place. Using a walking foot, stitch around all 4 sides, leaving a 6" opening on the opposite side of the appliquéd pieces for turning. Trim the corners and turn the mantel banner right side out. Gently push out the corners with a point turner. Slipstitch the opening closed, and topstitch ¼" away from the edges on all sides.

9. Sew a tassel to the point of each appliquéd piece.

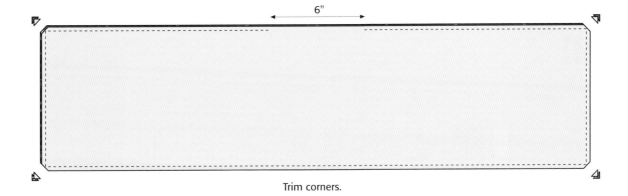

6"

Trim corners.

"SNOWFLAKE" TISSUE-BOX COVER

Finished tissue-box-cover size: 4½" x 4½" x 5¾"

CUTTING

All measurements include ¼"-wide seam allowances.

From medium blue #1, cut:
- 2 rectangles, 6" x 7", for sides
- 1 square, 6" x 6", for top

From the light blue, cut:
- 2 rectangles, 6" x 7", for sides

From medium blue #2, cut:
- 2 strips, 2¼" x 6", for top opening binding
- 1 strip, 2¼" x 19", for bottom binding

From the muslin, cut:
- 4 rectangles, 8" x 9", for side backing
- 1 square, 8" x 8", for top backing

From the batting, cut:
- 4 rectangles, 8" x 9", for sides
- 1 square, 8" x 8", for top

ASSEMBLING THE TISSUE-BOX COVER

1. Referring to "Fusible-Web Appliqué" on pages 7–9, trace 4 of the appliqué pattern on page 59 onto the paper side of the fusible web. Cut around the shapes. Fuse 2 of the appliqué shapes onto the wrong side of the white fabric and 2 onto the wrong side of the remaining medium blue #2. Cut out the appliqués on the drawn lines and remove the paper backing. Be sure to cut out the 6 diamond shapes inside of each snowflake.

2. Center the white snowflakes on the 6" x 7" medium blue #1 background rectangles and the blue snowflakes on the 6" x 7" light blue rectangles. Fuse in place.

3. Machine stitch around the edges of each appliqué shape, using either a buttonhole stitch, satin stitch, or zigzag stitch.

4. Place a batting 8" x 9" rectangle over each muslin 8" x 9" rectangle. Center an appliquéd rectangle on top of each batting rectangle, right side up; pin baste the layers together. Quilt as desired. Trim each quilted piece to 5" x 6", keeping the design centered.

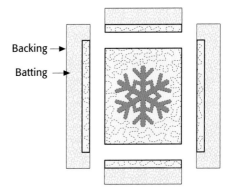

NOTE: *The batting and backing are cut larger than the appliquéd rectangles to simplify maneuvering the layers under the presser foot while quilting close to the outside edges.*

5. Place the batting 8" square over the muslin 8" square. Center the 6" medium blue #1 square over the batting square, right side up; pin the layers together. Quilt as desired. Trim the square to 5" x 5". Cut the quilted piece in half to make 2 rectangles, 2½" x 5".

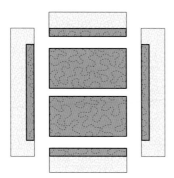

6. Press the 2¼" x 6" medium blue #2 strips in half lengthwise, wrong sides together. Align the raw edges of each strip with one long edge of each rectangle from step 5; stitch in place. Referring to "Binding the Edges" on page 13, steps 12 and 13, fold the binding strips to the back, encasing the raw edges, and pin in place. Stitch in the ditch to secure the binding. Trim the raw edges of the binding even with the quilted fabric.

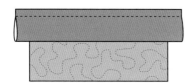

7. Butt the bound edges together; baste, using a whipstitch to keep the edges closed. Verify that the top of the box cover measures 5" square and trim if necessary, keeping the bound edges centered. On the wrong side of the top, place a mark ¼" in from each side of each corner.

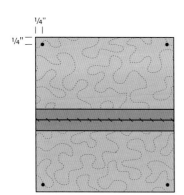

8. Sew the 4 side panels together along the 6" edges to form a strip, alternating light and dark rectangles. Press seams open.

9. Press the 2¼" x 19" binding strip in half lengthwise, wrong sides together. With raw edges even, stitch the binding to one long side of the quilted side panels. Refer to step 6 to finish the binding. Trim the binding edges even with the ends of the quilted side panels.

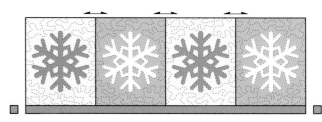

Trim binding.

10. Fold the side panel strip in half widthwise, right sides together; stitch the short ends together, beginning at the bound edge, to create a tube. Backstitch at the beginning and end of the stitching line. Do not turn right side out.

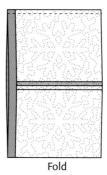

Fold

11. Place the top unit of the box cover inside the tube, right sides together, along one of the side panels. Align the corner marks with the seam lines of the side panel and pin in place. Stitch between the marks, backstitching at the beginning and end. Remove from the machine and clip the threads.

Repeat the process on all 4 sides, aligning each side of the top with the corresponding side panel. Trim the corners and turn right side out, pushing out the corners with a point turner.

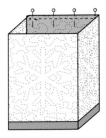

12. Remove the basting stitches from the top of the box cover.

"Snowflake" Tissue-Box Cover
Appliqué Pattern

"THINK SNOW!" DOOR TOPPER

Finished door-topper size: 12" x 24"

MATERIALS

Yardage is based on 42"-wide fabric.

- ✦ ⅜ yard of light blue print for background top
- ✦ ¼ yard of white for snowman and background bottom
- ✦ 5" x 5" square of green plaid for vest
- ✦ 5" x 5" square of red-on-red stripe for hat border and scarf
- ✦ 3" x 4" rectangle of off-white for sign
- ✦ 1" x 5" rectangle of wood print for signpost
- ✦ Scrap of red print for hat
- ✦ Scrap of red print suitable for pom-pom
- ✦ Scrap of orange for nose

- ✦ Scraps of 3 assorted greens for tree sections
- ✦ ⅝ yard of fabric for backing and hanging sleeves
- ✦ ½ yard of dark blue for binding
- ✦ 15" x 27" rectangle of batting
- ✦ 11" x 11" square of paper-backed fusible web
- ✦ Black permanent-ink fabric marker
- ✦ Appliqué pressing sheet
- ✦ 6 black ⅛"-diameter buttons for snowman mouth and eyes
- ✦ ½"-diameter wooden dowels: 8" long and 23" long

CUTTING

All measurements include ¼"-wide seam allowances.

From the light blue, cut:

+ 1 rectangle, 9½" x 12", for snowman background
+ 2 rectangles, 3½" x 7½", for sides
+ 2 rectangles, 3½" x 5½", for tops of A-B trees
+ 1 rectangle, 2¼" x 3½", for top of A-B-C tree

From the white, cut:

+ 1 strip, 1½" x 24½", for snow

From the backing fabric, cut:

+ 1 rectangle, 15" x 27"
+ 1 strip, 3½" x 8"
+ 1 strip, 3½" x 24"

ASSEMBLING THE DOOR TOPPER

1. Referring to "Paper Piecing" on pages 10 and 11, copy or trace the foundation patterns on page 21 onto foundation paper. Make 3 patterns *each* of units A and B. Make 1 pattern of unit C, using the alternate cutting line at the bottom of the pattern. Paper piece each unit, referring to the pattern for the appropriate fabric to use in each section of each unit.

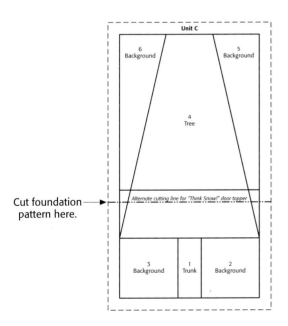

2. After all the pieces have been added, trim only the edges of each unit that will be joined to another unit. Stitch each A unit to a B unit. Stitch the C unit to one of the A-B units. Remove the paper from the seam allowances only. Press the seams toward the tops of the trees. Turn the blocks to the paper side. Trim the A-B blocks to 3½" x 7" and the A-B-C block to 3½" x 10¼" along the outside dotted lines. Do not remove the paper foundation until the blocks are set into the project. This will eliminate any stretching that can occur when the bias edges are handled.

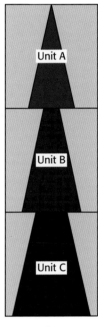

Make 2.

Make 1.

3. Sew the foundation-pieced units from step 2 and the light blue rectangles together as shown below. Press the seams toward the background pieces. Stitch the white strip to the bottom of the background unit. Press the seam toward the white strip.

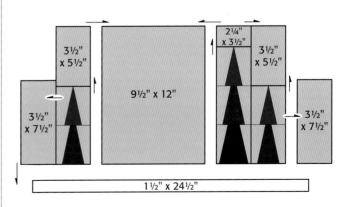

4. Referring to "Block 9: Snowman" on page 37, step 2, make the snowman appliqué unit. Place the snowman unit on the pieced background unit, centering the bottom of the snowman 1⅜" from each side seam of the background center rectangle and positioning the bottom corners of the snowman even with the snow seam. Fuse in place.

5. Mark the stitching detail line on the snowman vest. Satin stitch along the detail line. Machine stitch around the edges of each appliqué shape, using either a buttonhole stitch, satin stitch, or zigzag stitch.

6. Place the 15" x 27" backing rectangle on a flat surface, wrong side up. Layer the batting rectangle on top of the backing rectangle. Center the appliquéd top on the batting rectangle, right side up, and pin baste. Quilt as desired.

7. To make the template for the door topper, copy or trace each of the patterns on pages 65–67 onto a separate piece of paper. Matching the corresponding lines on Section I and Section II, tape the pieces of paper together. Align and tape Section III to the top of Sections I and II, matching the center lines. Cut out on the outside line.

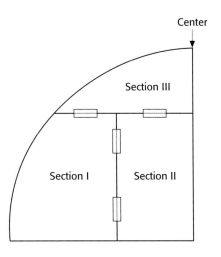

8. Fold the snowman unit in half along the long edges and place a pin at the center point on the top and bottom of the unit. Place the door-topper template on top of the quilted door topper, aligning the template center line with the pins and the template bottom edge with the bottom edge of the snow. Pin in place. Trace around the outside edges of the pattern with a pencil or fabric marker, stopping when you get to the center line. Turn the pattern over and repeat for the other half of the door topper. Remove the template and cut out the door topper along the drawn lines.

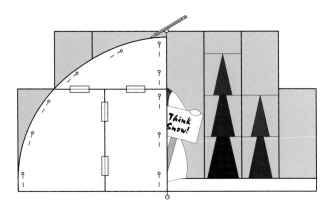

9. To make the bias binding, fold the selvage edge of the binding fabric up diagonally to form a triangle. Align the edges.

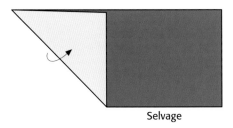

Selvage

Rotate the fabric on the cutting mat so that the folded edge is facing you. Place an acrylic ruler on the triangle with the long edge perpendicular to the fold. Position the ruler so that one of the horizontal lines on the ruler is aligned with the fabric fold and the long edge of the ruler intersects the point of the triangle. Cut off the corner triangle of the fabric and set aside.

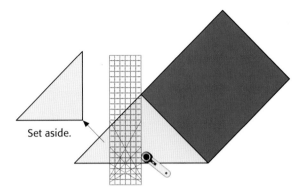

Set aside.

Open out the fabric and cut 3 strips, each 2½" wide, from the bias edge of the fabric. The ends of each strip should be at a 45° angle.

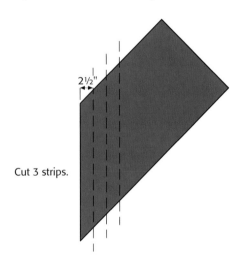

2½"

Cut 3 strips.

Sew the 3 strips together to make one long strip. Press the strip in half lengthwise, wrong sides together.

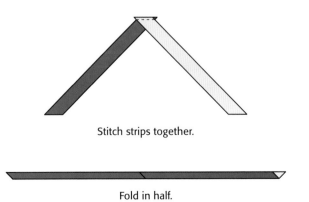

Stitch strips together.

Fold in half.

10. Cut a 26" length from the binding strip; set it aside. With raw edges aligned and the binding strip centered, stitch the remaining length of binding strip to the right side of the door-topper curved edge. Referring to "Binding the Edges" on page 13, steps 12 and 13, fold the binding strip to the back, encasing the raw edges, and pin in place. Stitch in the ditch to secure the binding. Trim the ends even with the bottom of the door topper.

11. With raw edges even and the binding strip centered, stitch the 26" length of binding strip to the right side of the door-topper lower edge. Trim the ends ¼" longer than the sides of the door topper. Fold the ends in before turning the binding over and stitching down as in step 10.

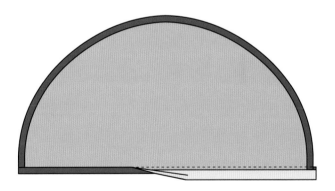

12. Stitch the buttons to the snowman's head where indicated for the eyes and mouth.

13. Using the remaining backing strips, make 2 hanging sleeves for the topper, referring to "Attaching a Hanging Sleeve" on page 15. Center the shorter sleeve ¾" from the top of the door topper and hand stitch in place. Center the longer sleeve along the bottom binding of the door topper and hand stitch in place. Insert the 8" dowel in the top sleeve for hanging and the 23" dowel in the bottom sleeve to keep the door topper hanging flat against the wall.

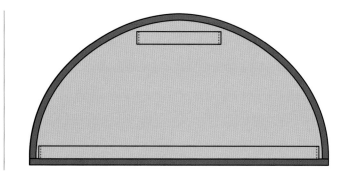

"Think Snow!" Door Topper
Pattern

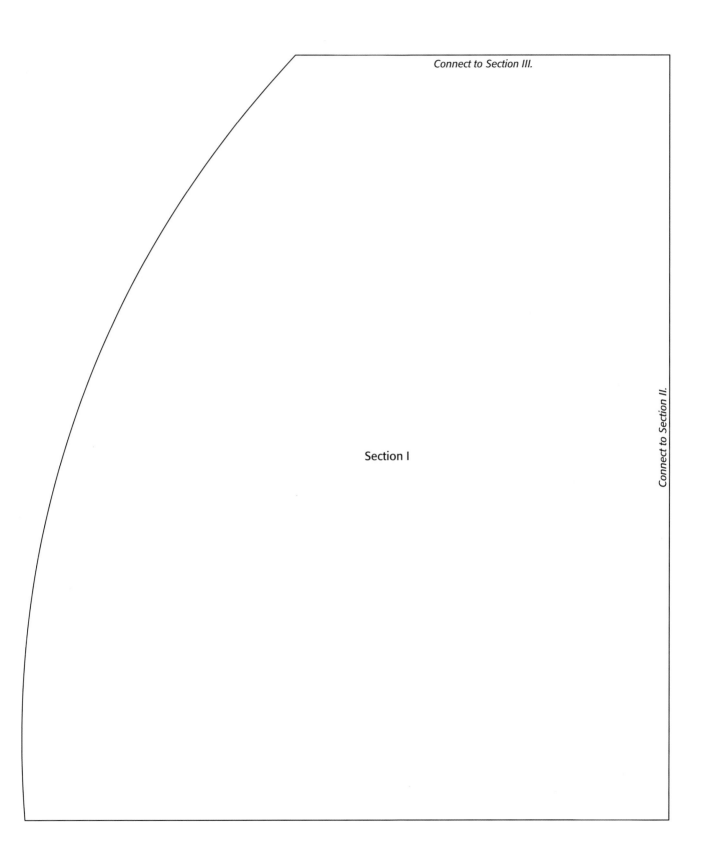

Connect to Section III.

Connect to Section II.

Section I

"Think Snow!" Door Topper
Pattern

Connect to Section III.

Connect to Section I.

Section II

Center

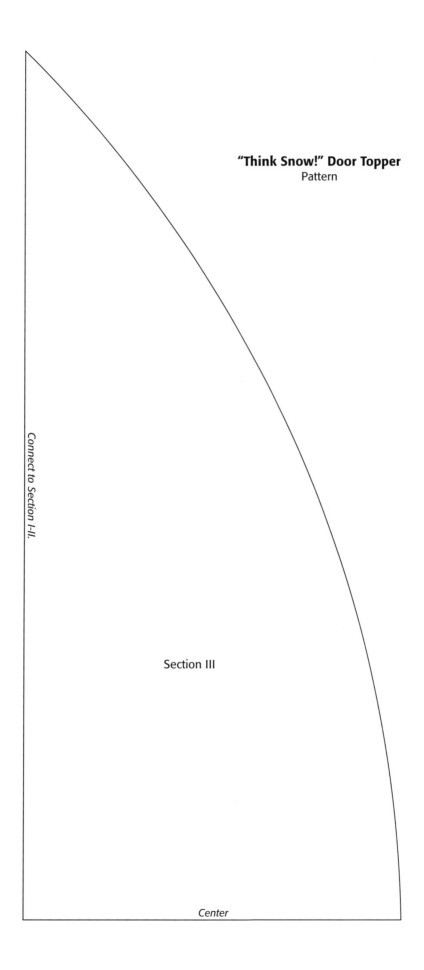

"Think Snow!" Door Topper
Pattern

Connect to Section I-II.

Section III

Center

"PATCHWORK MITTENS" MITTEN DRYER

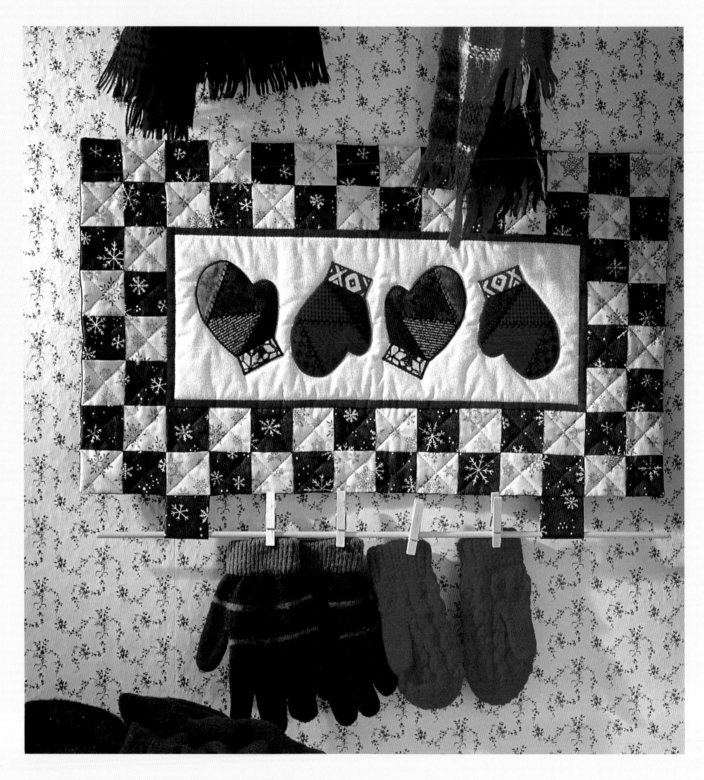

Finished mitten-dryer size: 13" x 22"

CUTTING

All measurements include ¼"-wide seam allowances.

From the cream, cut:
- ◆ 1 strip, 6½" x 15½", for center

From the red for inner border, cut:
- ◆ 2 strips, ¾" x 42". Crosscut to make:
    - 2 strips, ¾" x 6½", for inner side borders
    - 2 strips, ¾" x 15", for inner top and bottom borders

From the tan, cut:
- ◆ 2 strips, 2" x 42", for outer border

From the dark blue, cut:
- ◆ 2 strips, 2" x 42", for outer border
- ◆ 1 strip, 3½" x 8", for tabs
- ◆ 1 rectangle, 12½" x 21½", for backing

ASSEMBLING THE MITTEN DRYER

1. Referring to "Paper Piecing" on pages 10 and 11, use the pattern on page 72 to copy or trace 2 mitten foundation patterns and 2 reverse mitten foundation patterns. Paper piece 1 foundation pattern and 1 reverse foundation pattern using the 5 coordinating red fabrics; trim the seams to ⅛" after each addition. Repeat with the remaining foundation patterns and the 5 coordinating blue fabrics. After adding all the pieces, trim the foundation squares along the pattern outer edges and remove the paper from the back of the block.

2. Referring to "Fusible-Web Appliqué" on pages 7–9, use the appliqué pattern on page 72 to trace 2 mittens and 2 reverse mittens onto the paper side of the fusible web. Be sure to trace the inner lines onto the mittens. Cut around the shapes.

3. Place the foundation-pieced squares on the ironing board, wrong side up. Position each fusible-web shape on a square, aligning the lines on the shape with the fabric seams. Fuse the shapes in place.

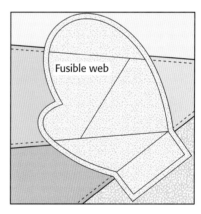

Align traced lines over
foundation seam lines.

4. Cut out the appliqués on the outer drawn lines and remove the paper backing.

5. Place the cream 6½" x 15½" strip on the ironing board, right side up. Arrange the appliqués on the strip as shown, placing the first and last appliqués 1¼" from the side edges and centering all 4 appliqués within the rectangle. Fuse the appliqués in place.

6. With a decorative machine stitch and contrasting thread, stitch over the seams of each mitten if desired. Machine stitch around the edges of each appliqué shape, using either a buttonhole stitch, satin stitch, or zigzag stitch.

7. Trim the appliquéd strip to 6" x 15", keeping the design centered.

8. Stitch the red ¾" x 15" strips to the top and bottom edges of the appliquéd strip. Trim the seams to ⅛" and press toward the border strips. Stitch the red ¾" x 6½" strips to the sides of the appliquéd strip. Trim the seam allowances to ⅛" and press toward the border strips.

9. Sew each tan 2" x 42" strip to a dark blue 2" x 42" strip along the long edges. Press the seams toward the blue strips. Make 2. From the strip sets, cut a total of 36 segments, each 2" wide.

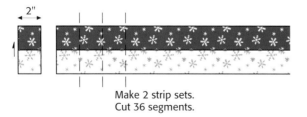

Make 2 strip sets.
Cut 36 segments.

10. Sew 2 segments together as shown to make a four-patch unit. Press the seam to one side. Make 18.

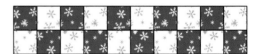

Make 18.

11. To make the outer-border strips for the top and bottom of the mitten dryer, sew 5 four-patch units together, placing a dark square in the upper-left corner as shown. Press seams in one direction. Make 2.

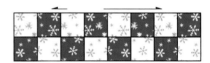

Outer Top and Bottom Border Strips
Make 2.

12. To make the outer-border strips for the sides of the mitten dryer, sew 4 four-patch units together, placing a light square in the upper-left corner as shown. Press the seam on the far left to the left. Press the remaining seams to the right. Make 2.

Outer Side Border Strips
Make 2.

13. Stitch the top and bottom outer-border strips to the top and bottom edges of the mitten dryer. Press the seams toward the inner border. Stitch the side outer-border strips to the sides of the mitten dryer. Press the seams toward the inner border.

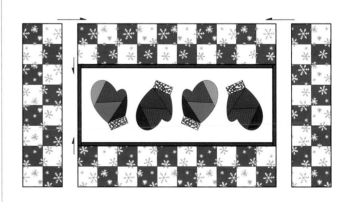

14. To make the hanging tabs, fold the dark blue 3½" x 8" strip in half lengthwise, right sides together. Stitch along the long raw edges. Position the seam allowance in the center of the tube. Using just the tip of the iron, gently press the seam open. Be careful not to crease the edges of the tube as you press. Turn the tube right side out. With the seam allowance positioned in the center of the tube, press the tube flat. Cut the tube into 2 segments, each 3½".

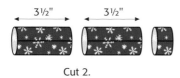

Cut 2.

15. Fold each segment in half so that the seam is on the inside and the raw edges are aligned.

16. Pin the folded segments to the bottom edge of the mitten-dryer top as shown, aligning the tab and pieced-border raw edges, and positioning each segment 3¼" from the sides. Using a scant ¼" seam allowance, machine baste the tabs in place from just outside the left-hand tab to just beyond the right-hand tab without breaking the stitching line between them.

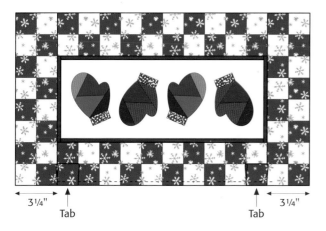

FINISHING THE MITTEN DRYER

1. Lay the completed mitten-dryer top, right side up, over the batting rectangle. With right sides together, place the backing rectangle over the mitten-dryer top. Pin the layers together.

2. Using a walking foot, stitch around the edges of the layered unit, leaving a 6" opening along the bottom edge between the tabs for turning. Backstitch at the beginning and end of the stitching line.

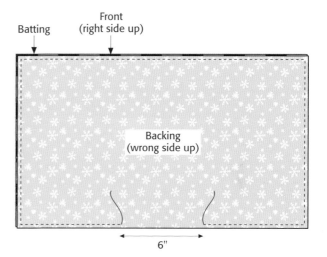

3. Trim the corners to reduce bulk. Turn to the right side through the opening. Gently push out the edges and corners with a point turner. Lightly press the edges of the unit so the mitten dryer remains flat. Slipstitch the opening closed.

4. Refer to "Quilting" on page 13 to quilt the mitten dryer as desired.

5. Refer to "Attaching a Hanging Sleeve" on page 15 to add a hanging sleeve to the mitten dryer. Insert the dowel through the tabs at the bottom of the dryer. Use the miniature clothespins to attach purchased mittens.

"Patchwork Mittens" Mitten Dryer

Foundation Pattern

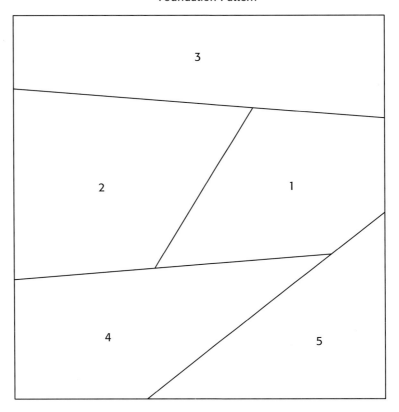

Appliqué Pattern

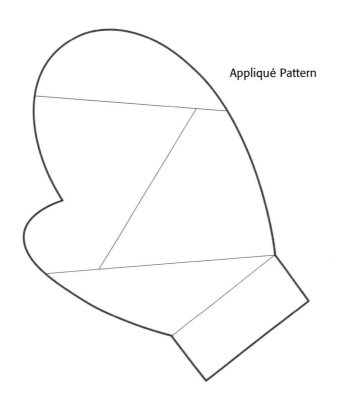

"SKATES AND FLAKES" PILLOW SHAM

Finished pillow-sham size: 18" x 18"

MATERIALS

Yardage is based on 42"-wide fabric.

- 1 yard of medium blue #1 for sashing, borders, Prairie Points, and sham back
- ⅜ yard of light blue snowflake print for background
- 7" x 13" rectangle of medium blue #2 for snowflakes
- 5" x 7" rectangle of white for skates
- 2" x 4" rectangle of black for skate heels
- 3" x 6" rectangle of gray for skate blades
- ⅝ yard of muslin for sham-top backing
- 18" x 18" square of batting
- 1 yard of ⅛"-wide white double-faced satin ribbon for laces
- 12" x 12" square of paper-backed fusible web
- Appliqué pressing sheet
- Black embroidery thread for soles
- 12" to 14" throw pillow or pillow form

CUTTING

All measurements include ¼"-wide seam allowances.

From the light blue snowflake print, cut:
- 4 squares, 7" x 7", for appliqué backgrounds

From medium blue #1, cut:
- 1 strip, 1½" x 42". Crosscut to make:
  2 strips, 1½" x 6½", for sashing
  1 strip, 1½" x 13½", for sashing
- 2 strips, 1¾" x 42". Crosscut to make:
  2 strips, 1¾" x 13½", for side borders
  2 strips, 1¾" x 16", for top and bottom borders
- 2 rectangles, 11" x 16", for sham back
- 2 strips, 7" x 42". Crosscut to make:
  4 strips, 7" x 15¾", for Prairie Points

From the muslin, cut:
- 1 square, 20" x 20", for sham-top backing

ASSEMBLING THE PILLOW-SHAM TOP

1. Referring to "Block 11: Snowflake" on page 45, make 2 Snowflake blocks, using medium blue #2 for the snowflake appliqué and the snowflake-print 7" squares for the background. Trim each block to 6½" x 6½", keeping the design centered.

2. Referring to step 1 of "Block 5: Ice Skates" on page 26, use the pattern on page 77 to make 1 ice-skate appliqué unit and 1 reverse ice-skate appliqué unit. Center each skate on one of the remaining snowflake-print 7" squares, referring to the photo on page 73 for the placement angle. Fuse the appliqué units in place.

3. Mark the stitching detail lines on the ice skates for laces.

4. Machine stitch around the edges of each appliqué shape, using either a buttonhole stitch, satin stitch, or zigzag stitch. To make the soles of the ice skates, machine satin stitch along the bottom of each shoe, using black embroidery thread. Satin stitch over the lace detail lines, using a narrow satin stitch and white thread.

5. Trim each block to 6½" x 6½", keeping the design centered.

6. Arrange the blocks and 1½" x 6½" medium blue #1 strips into 2 vertical rows as shown. Stitch the blocks and sashing strips together in each row. Press seam allowances toward the sashing strips. Stitch the 1½" x 13½" medium blue #1 strip between the rows. Press seams toward the sashing strip.

7. Stitch the 1¾" x 13½" medium blue #1 strips to the sides of the sham top. Press seams toward the border strips. Stitch the 1¾" x 16" medium blue #1 strips to the top and bottom of the sham top. Press seams toward the border strips.

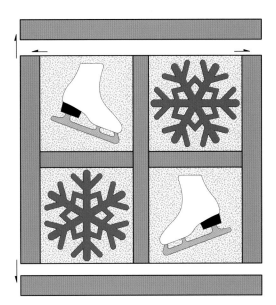

FINISHING THE PILLOW SHAM

1. Refer to "Project Finishing" on pages 12–15 to layer the sham top, the batting, and the 20" muslin square. Baste and quilt. Trim the backing and batting even with the edges of the sham top.

2. Press under ¼" along one long side of each of the 11" x 16" sham-back rectangles. Press under ¼" again and stitch the edges in place.

3. Place the sham-back rectangles on a flat surface, wrong sides up. Overlap the finished ends 5", keeping the top and bottom edges of each rectangle aligned as shown. Verify that the piece measures 16" x 16". Make any necessary adjustments, and then pin the overlapped edges together. Machine

baste the raw edges together using a scant ¼" seam allowance.

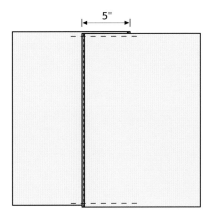

Baste in place.

4. Make the Prairie Point borders by pressing 1 of the 7" x 15¾" medium blue #1 strips in half lengthwise, wrong sides together. Open out the strip and place it, wrong side up, on a flat surface. Beginning on the left side of the center crease, measure 3½" up from the bottom edge and draw a horizontal line to the center crease. Repeat 3 more times. There should now be 4 squares, 3½" x 3½", drawn to the left of the center crease, with a 1¾" x 3½" rectangle at the top. Cut away the 1¾" rectangle. Turn the fabric strip 180° so that the unmarked side of the crease is on the left and repeat the above procedure. Cut along the drawn lines on both sides up to, but not past, the center crease.

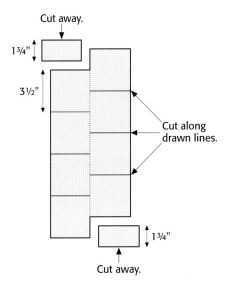

NOTE: *Use scissors for this procedure, because they offer more control than a rotary cutter. It is important that you do not cut past the center crease.*

5. Transfer the fabric rectangle to the ironing board. Beginning with the lower-left square, bring the left corner up to the center crease, forming a right triangle; press. Fold the triangle in half by bringing the left point down and press again. Insert a pin to hold the points of the triangle together.

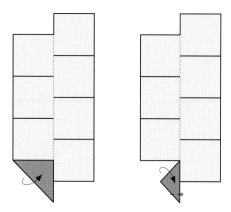

6. Working on the right-hand side, bring the right corner up to the center crease, forming a right triangle; press. Flip the first triangle over so that the point faces to the right and press. Fold the second triangle in half by bringing the right point down and press again. Insert a pin to hold the points of the triangle together.

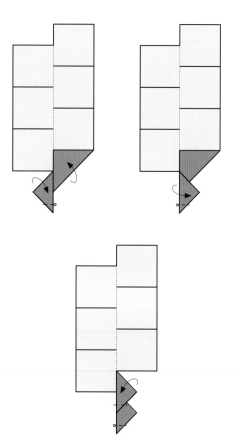

7. Repeat steps 5 and 6, alternating sides, until all the cut squares have been folded into triangles and pinned in place. Baste the raw edges of the Prairie Point chain, using a scant ¼" seam allowance. Repeat with the remaining three 7" x 15¾" medium blue #1 strips.

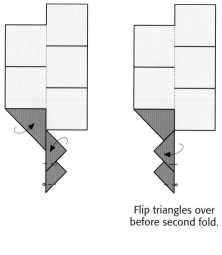

Flip triangles over before second fold.

8. Baste a Prairie Point strip to the top and bottom edges of the sham top and then to the sides.

9. Pin the sham top and back right sides together. Stitch around all 4 sides. Trim the corners. Turn the sham to the right side through the opening in the back. Push out the corners with a point turner. Lightly press the edges of the pillow sham.

10. Cut the ribbon into 2 equal lengths. Make a small bow at the center of each length. Tack one bow to each skate where indicated, and trim excess ribbon as desired. Be sure to sew through the knot. This will secure the ribbon and prevent the bow from coming untied. The ribbon tails also may be tacked to the sham top to keep them in place.

11. Insert the throw pillow or pillow form into the sham.

"Skates and Flakes" Pillow Sham
Appliqué Patterns

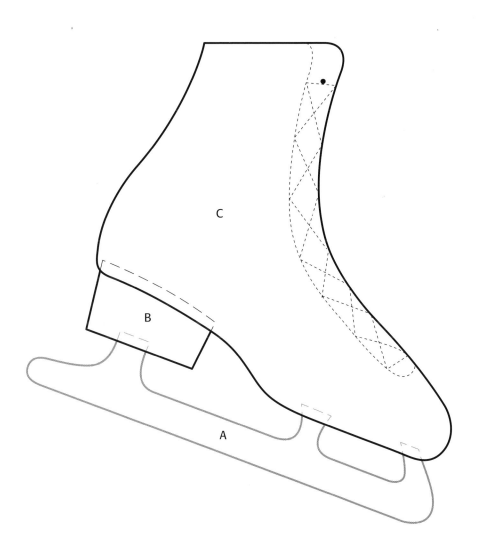

"WINTER WELCOME" WALL HANGING

Finished wall-hanging size: 13" x 18"

MATERIALS

Yardage is based on 42"-wide fabric.

- ⅝ yard or 1 fat quarter of wood-grain print for borders*
- ⅜ yard or 1 fat quarter of cream for background
- 8" x 10" rectangle of black for letters and sled
- 7" x 9" rectangle of red barn board print for sled
- ½ yard of fabric for backing
- 13½" x 18½" rectangle of batting
- 10" x 11" rectangle of paper-backed fusible web
- Appliqué pressing sheet

You will need at least a 16" length of fabric that runs with the grain of the wood.

CUTTING

All measurements include ¼"-wide seam allowances.

From the cream, cut:
- 1 rectangle, 10" x 14", for appliqué background

From the wood-grain print, cut:
- 3 strips, 2½" x 13½", for side and bottom borders
- 1 strip, 3½" x 13½", for top border

From the backing fabric, cut:
- 1 rectangle, 13½" x 18½"

The wood border will look more natural if the strips are all cut with the grain of the wood running lengthwise.

ASSEMBLING THE WALL HANGING

1. Referring to "Block 3: Sled" on page 22, step 1, make 1 sled appliqué unit.

2. Fold the cream rectangle in half lengthwise and finger-press along the fold. Open the rectangle and place the sled appliqué unit 1" from the bottom edge, centering the center board of the sled over the center crease. Fuse the appliqué in place.

3. Referring to "Fusible-Web Appliqué" on pages 7–9, trace the appliqué patterns on page 82 onto the paper side of the fusible web. Trace 1 each of A–U. Cut around the shapes. Fuse each appliqué shape to the wrong side of the black fabric. Cut out the appliqués on the drawn lines. Because some of the appliqués look similar, keep the paper backing in place for now so that you can refer to the pattern letters later if necessary.

4. Use the pattern on page 82 to make a placement diagram for the letters. Place the placement diagram on the ironing board. Place the appliquéd rectangle on top of the placement diagram so that the tops of the letters are 1" from the top edge and the center of the letter "C" is over the center crease. Stick a few straight pins into the ironing-board cover through the appliquéd rectangle and placement diagram to prevent shifting. Remove the paper backing on each appliqué shape just before placing it on the background rectangle. Fuse the appliqués in place one piece at a time.

5. Machine stitch around the edges of each appliqué shape, using a buttonhole stitch, satin stitch, or zigzag stitch.

6. Trim the completed background rectangle to 9½" x 13½", keeping the design centered.

7. Sew a 2½" x 13½" wood-grain strip to the sides of the appliquéd rectangle. Press the seams toward the borders. Sew the remaining 2½" x 13½" wood-grain strip to the bottom of the appliquéd rectangle. Press the seam toward the border.

8. To make the top border strip, copy or trace the top-border template on page 82. Cut out on the line. Fold the 3½" x 13½" wood-grain strip in half width-wise. Pin the top-border template to the fabric strip, aligning the wide end along the fold. Cut out on the line.

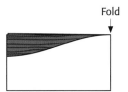

Fold

9. Place the straight edge of the top-border strip along the top edge of the appliquéd background rectangle and stitch in place. Press the seam toward the border.

FINISHING THE WALL HANGING

1. Fold the backing rectangle in half lengthwise, right sides together. Place the top-border template on the top edge of the backing rectangle so that the curved edge is adjacent to the top edge of the fabric and the side edges are even. Pin in place. Cut along the curved edge of the template. Remove the template and press the backing rectangle open.

Fold

2. Repeat step 1 with the batting rectangle. Open the batting rectangle and place on a flat surface. Place the backing rectangle on top of the batting, right side up. Align the backing and batting edges and smooth out any wrinkles.

3. Place the appliquéd top wrong side up over the backing. Carefully pin all of the layers together.

4. Using a walking foot, stitch the layers together around all sides, leaving a 5" opening at the bottom for turning; backstitch at the beginning and end of the stitching line.

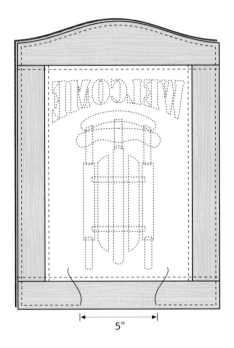

5. Trim the corner seam allowances to reduce bulk. Turn the wall hanging to the right side through the opening. Gently push the corners out with a point turner. Lightly press the edges so the wall hanging remains flat. Slipstitch the opening closed.

6. Quilt as desired.

7. Refer to "Attaching a Hanging Sleeve" on page 15 to make and attach a sleeve for hanging.

The wall hanging in the photo was simply quilted around each appliqué shape, not in the background. If too much quilting is done without quilting the borders also, it will cause the borders to be wavy and the wall hanging will not hang flat.

"Winter Welcome" Wall Hanging

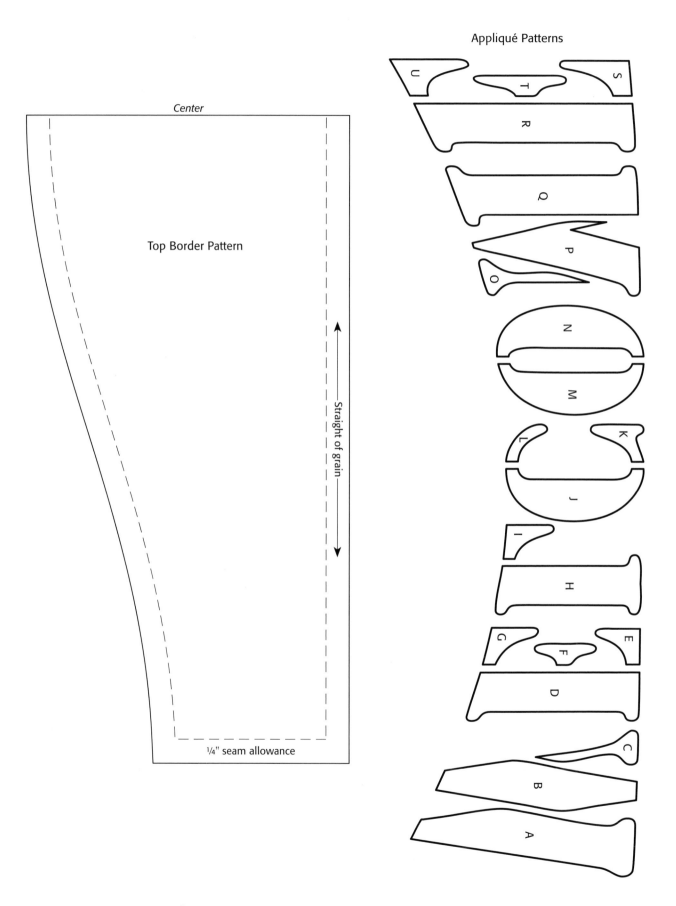

Appliqué Patterns

Center

Top Border Pattern

Straight of grain

¼" seam allowance

"WINTER CABIN" TABLE TOPPER

Finished table-topper size: 45" x 45"

CUTTING

All measurements include ¼"-wide seam allowances.

From the tan print, cut:

- ✦ 2 strips, 2" x 42"; crosscut into 8 rectangles, 2" x 8¼"
- ✦ 1 strip, 1¾" x 42"; crosscut into 4 rectangles, 1¾" x 9½"
- ✦ 4 strips, 1½" x 42". Crosscut into:
    - 4 rectangles, 1½" x 8½"
    - 4 rectangles, 1½" x 7½"
    - 4 rectangles, 1½" x 6½"
    - 4 rectangles, 1½" x 5½"
    - 4 rectangles, 1½" x 4½"
    - 4 rectangles, 1½" x 3½"
    - 4 rectangles, 1½" x 2½"
    - 4 squares, 1½" x 1½"

From the red, cut:

- ✦ 1 rectangle, 1½" x 15"; crosscut into 9 squares, 1½" x 1½"
- ✦ 1 rectangle, 1⅞" x 16"; crosscut into 8 squares, 1⅞" x 1⅞"

From the assorted blue fabrics, cut a *total* of:

- ✦ 8 rectangles, 1½" x 9⅞"
- ✦ 8 rectangles, 1½" x 8⅞"
- ✦ 8 rectangles, 1½" x 7⅞"
- ✦ 8 rectangles, 1½" x 6⅞"
- ✦ 8 rectangles, 1½" x 5⅞"
- ✦ 8 rectangles, 1½" x 4⅞"
- ✦ 8 rectangles, 1½" x 3⅞"
- ✦ 8 rectangles, 1½" x 2⅞"
- ✦ 9 rectangles, 1½" x 9½"
- ✦ 14 rectangles, 1½" x 8½"
- ✦ 14 rectangles, 1½" x 7½"
- ✦ 14 rectangles, 1½" x 6½"
- ✦ 14 rectangles, 1½" x 5½"
- ✦ 14 rectangles, 1½" x 4½"
- ✦ 14 rectangles, 1½" x 3½"
- ✦ 14 rectangles, 1½" x 2½"
- ✦ 5 squares, 1½" x 1½"

From the backing fabric, cut:

- ✦ 2 rectangles, 42" x 47"

From the dark blue, cut:

- ✦ 4 strips, 2½" x 42", for binding

ASSEMBLING THE TABLE-TOPPER TOP

1. Referring to steps 1 and 2 of "Block 8: Winter Cabin" on page 34, paper piece 4 Winter Cabin blocks. Sew a tan 2" x 8¼" rectangle to both sides of each block. Press the seams toward the tan rectangles. Sew a tan 1¾" x 9½" rectangle to the bottom of each block. Press the seam toward the tan rectangle. Remove the paper from each of the blocks. Continue with steps 4 and 5 of "Block 8: Winter Cabin" to complete the 4 Winter Cabin blocks. Set aside.

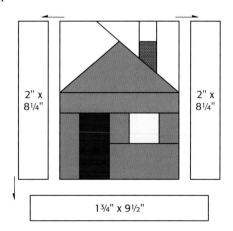

2" x 8¼" 2" x 8¼"

1¾" x 9½"

2. To make the blue Log Cabin blocks, stitch a red 1½" square to a blue 1½" square. Press the seam toward the red square. Stitch a blue 1½" x 2½" rectangle to opposite long sides of the red-and-blue unit. Press seams away from the center. Make 5 center units.

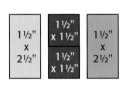 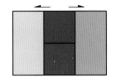

Make 5.

3. Using the blue 1½" x 3½" rectangles next, continue adding 2 blue rectangles of the same length to opposite sides of each center unit as shown, increasing the length each time by 1". After adding the 1½" x 8½" rectangles, stitch 1 blue 1½" x 9½" rectangle to the remaining side of the Log Cabin units so that the red square is now in the center of the block. Press seams away from the center unit after each addition. Make 5 blue Log Cabin blocks.

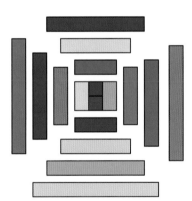

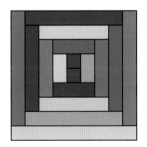

Make 5.

4. To make the blue-and-tan Log Cabin blocks, stitch a red 1½" square to a tan 1½" square. Press seams toward the red square. Stitch a tan 1½" x 2½" rectangle and a blue 1½" x 2½" rectangle to opposite long sides of the red-and-tan unit as shown. Press seams away from the center. Make 4 center units.

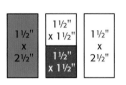 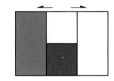

Make 4.

5. Continue adding 1 tan and 1 blue rectangle of the same length to opposite sides of each center unit as shown, increasing the length each time by 1". Be sure to sew all the blue rectangles on one half of the block and all the tan rectangles on the other half. After you have added the 1½" x 8½" rectangles, stitch 1 blue 1½" x 9½" rectangle to the remaining side of the Log Cabin units so that the red square is now in the center of the block. Press seams away from the center unit after each addition. Make 4 blue-and-tan Log Cabin blocks.

 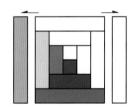

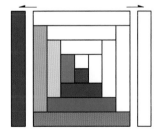 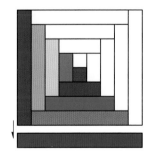

Make 4.

6. To make the Half Log Cabin blocks, stitch a red 1⅞" square to a blue 1½" x 2⅞" rectangle, aligning one end of the blue rectangle with the red square. Press the seam toward the red square. Stitch a blue 1½" x 3⅞" rectangle to the side of the red square perpendicular to the first rectangle. Press the seam toward the red square. Make 8 center units.

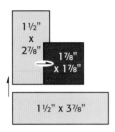

Make 8.

NOTE: *While it may seem natural to press the seams toward the newly added rectangles, in this block it is crucial to press the seams as indicated in the instructions. The uneven edges of the Half Log Cabin blocks will be trimmed after the block is completed; therefore, it is important to have the seam allowances extending along this edge.*

7. Continue alternately adding blue rectangles to the side and bottom of the center unit, increasing the length each time by 1". Press seams toward the center after each addition.

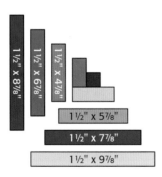

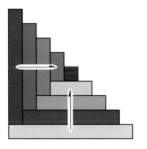

8. When all the rectangles have been added, place a ruler along the uneven edge of each block and trim off the points, leaving a straight edge. Make 8 Half Log Cabin blocks.

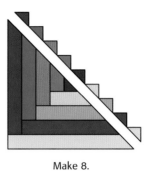

Make 8.

NOTE: *The blocks now have bias edges. Handle carefully so as not to distort their shape.*

9. Arrange the blocks into 5 horizontal rows as shown. Stitch the blocks in each row together and press the seam allowances in the directions indicated. Stitch the rows together. Press the seam allowances in the directions indicated.

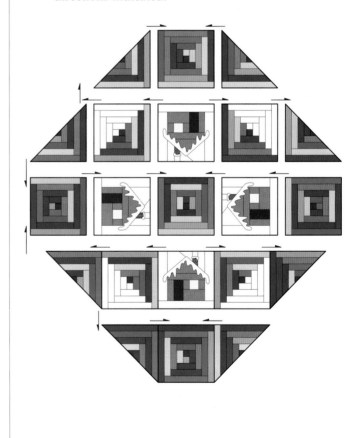

FINISHING
THE TABLE TOPPER

1. Referring to "Project Finishing" on pages 12–15, layer and quilt the table topper.

2. Stitch the binding to the edges of the table topper, mitering the corners as shown.

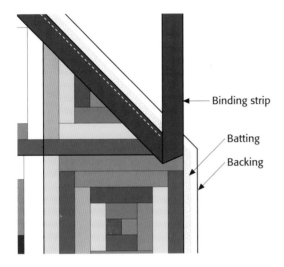

→ Binding strip

→ Batting
→ Backing

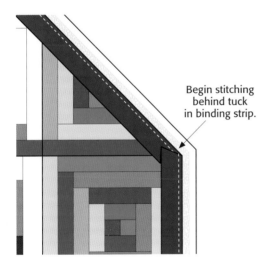

Begin stitching behind tuck in binding strip.

3. Trim the batting and backing ⅜" from the *stitching line*. Fold the binding to the back and stitch it in place.

 The snowflake quilting pattern that can be seen in the photo on page 83 was created using the snowflake template on page 46. Enlarge the template by 150% and then connect the outer lines of the diamond shapes to make one continuous line as shown in the illustration below. Center the snowflake quilting template within the Log Cabin and Half Log Cabin blocks and mark using your favorite technique. Do not stitch along dotted llines. Stitch in the ditch around the red center squares.

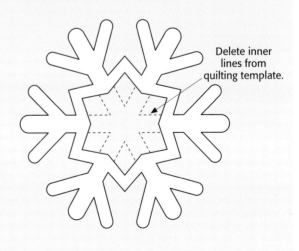

Delete inner lines from quilting template.

"WINTER VACANCY" WALL HANGING

Finished wall-hanging size: 15½" x 24½".

MATERIALS

Yardage is based on 42"-wide fabric.

- ✦ ½ yard of light blue print for background
- ✦ ⅜ yard of medium blue snowflake print for borders
- ✦ 7" x 7" square of wood print #1 for birdhouse
- ✦ 6" x 8" rectangle of white for snow
- ✦ 1½" x 7" strip *each* of 6 assorted greens for holly leaves
- ✦ Scrap of wood print #2 for pole and perch
- ✦ Scrap of bright red for cardinal head and breast
- ✦ Scrap of dark red for cardinal tail and wings
- ✦ Scrap of black for hole and cardinal mask
- ✦ Scrap of gold for cardinal beak
- ✦ Scrap of brown for branch
- ✦ ⅝ yard of fabric for backing
- ✦ ⅜ yard of dark blue for binding
- ✦ 17" x 26" rectangle of batting
- ✦ Foundation paper
- ✦ 8" x 12" rectangle of paper-backed fusible web
- ✦ 1 black ³⁄₁₆"-diameter button for cardinal eye
- ✦ 7 red ⅜"-diameter buttons for holly berries

CUTTING

All measurements include ¼"-wide seam allowances.

From the medium blue, cut:
- ✦ 2 strips, 3½" x 42". Crosscut into:
    2 strips, 3½" x 18½", for top and
        bottom borders
    2 strips, 3½" x 15½", for side borders

From the backing fabric, cut:
- ✦ 1 rectangle, 17" x 26"

From the dark blue, cut:
- ✦ 3 strips, 2½" x 42", for binding

ASSEMBLING THE WALL-HANGING TOP

1. Referring to "Block 10: Cardinal" on page 40, steps 1 and 2, make 1 Cardinal block.

2. Referring to "Block 7: Birdhouse" on page 31, steps 1–4, make 1 Birdhouse block.

3. Sew the Birdhouse block to the left side of the Cardinal block. Press the seam toward the Cardinal block.

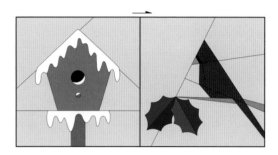

4. Sew a medium blue 3½" x 18½" strip to the top and bottom edges of the wall-hanging center. Press the seams toward the strips. Sew the medium blue 3½" x 15½" strips to the sides of the wall hanging. Press the seams toward the strips.

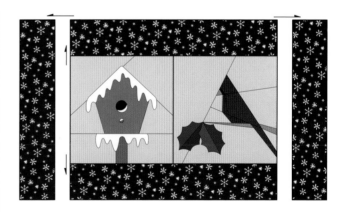

5. Referring to steps 3 and 4 of "Block 10: Cardinal" on page 41, stitch the assorted green 1½" x 7" strips together into pairs. Make 3. Trace 6 holly-leaf shapes using the pattern on page 25. Fuse 2 leaf shapes to each pieced strip. Cut out each leaf on the outside drawn lines and remove the paper backing.

6. Referring to the photo as a guide, arrange 2 of the leaves on the Cardinal block; fuse the leaves in place. Fuse 2 of each of the remaining leaves in both the upper-left corner and lower-right corner of the border, locating the intersection of the leaves 1¾" from each edge.

7. Machine stitch around the edges of each appliqué, using either a buttonhole stitch, satin stitch, or zigzag stitch.

FINISHING THE WALL HANGING

1. Refer to "Project Finishing" on pages 12–15 to layer, quilt, and bind the wall hanging.

2. After the wall hanging is completed, stitch the small black button to the bird's head where indicated for the eye. Stitch 3 of the red buttons in each corner between the holly leaves and 1 button on the branch where indicated for berries.

3. Refer to "Attaching a Hanging Sleeve" on page 15 to make and attach a sleeve for hanging.

"WINTERSCAPE" PLACE MATS

Finished place-mat size: 12" x 18"

MATERIALS

Yardage is based on 42"-wide fabric.
Materials listed are enough to make 4 place mats.

- ♦ ¾ yard of dark blue print for borders
- ♦ ½ yard of white snowflake print for background and stars
- ♦ ¼ yard of white solid for snow at bottom of tree
- ♦ ⅛ yard *each* of 3 assorted green prints for trees
- ♦ Scrap of brown for tree trunks
- ♦ 1 yard of fabric for backing
- ♦ ⅝ yard of navy blue for binding
- ♦ 1 yard of low-loft batting

CUTTING

All measurements include ¼"-wide seam allowances.

From the white snowflake print, cut:
- ♦ 1 strip, 6½" x 42". Crosscut to make:
    4 strips, 1½" x 6½"
    4 rectangles, 6½" x 7½"
- ♦ 1 strip, 1½" x 42". Crosscut to make:
    16 squares, 1½" x 1½", for Friendship Star centers
- ♦ 2 strips, 1⅞" x 42". Crosscut to make:
    32 squares, 1⅞" x 1⅞". Cut each square in half diagonally to make 64 half-square triangles for Friendship Star points.

From the white solid, cut:
- ♦ 2 strips, 1½" x 42". Crosscut to make:
    4 rectangles, 1½" x 2¾", for snow
    4 strips, 1½" x 8¾", for snow

From the brown, cut:
- ♦ 4 rectangles, 1" x 1½", for tree trunks

From the dark blue, cut:
- ♦ 2 strips, 3½" x 42"; crosscut to make 8 rectangles, 3½" x 5½", for side borders
- ♦ 3 strips, 2½" x 42"; crosscut to make 8 strips, 2½" x 11½", for top and bottom borders
- ♦ 3 strips, 1½" x 42"; crosscut to make 64 squares, 1½" x 1½", for Friendship Star corners
- ♦ 2 strips, 1⅞" x 42"; crosscut to make 32 squares, 1⅞" x 1⅞". Cut each square in half diagonally to make 64 half-square triangles for Friendship Star points.

From the backing fabric, cut:
- ♦ 2 strips, 14" x 42"; crosscut to make 4 rectangles, 14" x 20"

From the batting, cut:
- ♦ 4 rectangles, 14" x 20"

From the navy blue, cut:
- ♦ 7 strips, 2½" x 42", for binding

ASSEMBLING THE PLACE MATS

1. Using the patterns on page 94 and referring to the instructions for "Block 2: Evergreen Tree" on page 20, make 4 blocks. Trim each block to 3½" x 6½". Remove the paper from the back of each block.

2. Sew a 1½" x 6½" white print strip to the left-hand side of each block. Press the seams toward the white-print strips. Sew a 6½" x 7½" white print rectangle to the right-hand side of each block. Press the seams toward the rectangles.

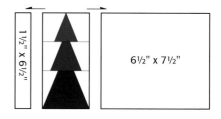

3. Sew each 1½" x 2¾" white solid rectangle to one side of a 1" x 1½" brown rectangle. Press the seams away from the brown rectangles. Sew a 1½" x 8¾" white solid strip to the opposite side of each brown rectangle. Press the seams away from the brown

rectangles. Make 4. Stitch a pieced strip to the bottom of each tree-block rectangle from step 2 as shown. Press the seams toward the pieced white strip.

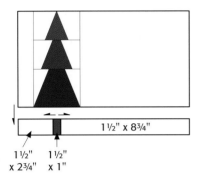

4. Sew the 2½" x 11½" dark blue strips to the top and bottom of each rectangle from step 3. Press the seams toward the borders.

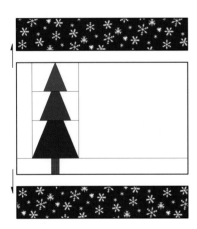

5. Refer to "Friendship Star Blocks" on page 47 to make 16 Friendship Star blocks. Sew a Friendship Star block to each short end of each 3½" x 5½" dark blue rectangle. Press the seams toward the rectangles. Stitch the pieced strips to the sides of each rectangle from step 4. Press the seams toward the center of each place mat.

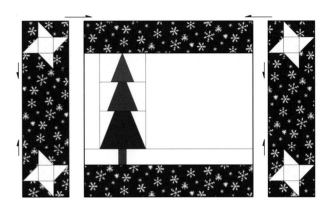

FINISHING THE PLACE MATS

Refer to "Project Finishing" on pages 12–15 to layer, quilt, and bind each place mat.

"Winterscape" Place Mats
Foundation Patterns

Unit A

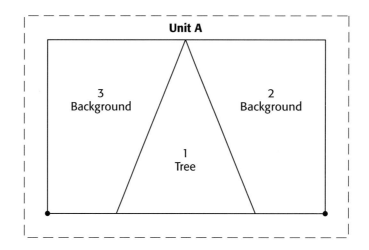

3
Background

2
Background

1
Tree

Unit B

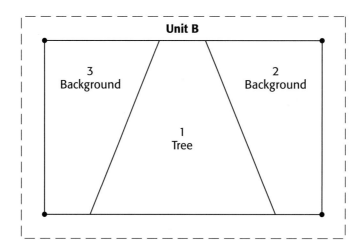

3
Background

2
Background

1
Tree

Unit C

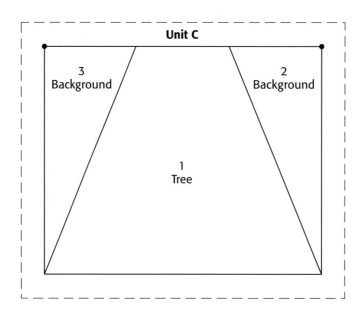

3
Background

2
Background

1
Tree

RESOURCES

Appliqué Pressing Sheet
Bear Thread Designs
PO Box 1452
Highlands, TX 77562
(281) 462-0661
www.bearthreaddesigns.com
beartd@hotmail.com

Clover White Marking Pen
Peace By Piece Designs
PO Box 350
Ashton, IL 61006
(866) 447-8458
www.PeaceByPieceDesigns.com

Miniature Clothespins
Crafts Etc.
7717 SW 44th Street
Oklahoma City, OK 73179
(405) 745-1200
(800) 888-0321
www.craftsetc.com

ABOUT THE AUTHOR

Lois Krushina Fletcher is a self-taught quilter who began quilting in 1990. After discovering that machine quilting was the answer to her lack of space because it required no frame, she began quilting in earnest. It quickly replaced her numerous other hobbies, becoming her passion and, eventually, her career. In 2000 she resigned from her full-time job with a major corporation to begin her own pattern-design company, Peace By Piece Designs. Since then, she has published several patterns as well as this book's predecessor, *The Quilter's Home: Fall*.

Lois has spent most of her life in the South, but an unexpected move in 2002 brought her to the small village of Ashton in northern Illinois. It is there that she now resides with her husband, four cats, and one dog. She has two grown sons, Michael and Matthew, who both still live in Texas. Although her move from her beloved Texas was not in her plans, she is enjoying her new life in the Midwest. She and her husband live in a home from 1914 that they are presently renovating. The third-floor walk-up attic will eventually become her studio, and with more than 600 square feet of space to work in, promises to be extremely comfortable. She has already warned her husband that she may never come down!

The move has allowed Lois to indulge in one of her other passions—gardening. She likes to grow both flowers and vegetables and finds canning and putting up preserves very relaxing and rewarding. When she is not working in the kitchen trying to keep up with her garden's bounty, she spends her time creating new designs for her ever-growing pattern line. You can see more of her patterns by visiting her Web site at www.PeaceByPieceDesigns.com.